LEARNING SPACES

YOUTH, LITERACY AND NEW MEDIA IN REMOTE INDIGENOUS AUSTRALIA

INGE KRAL &
ROBERT G. (JERRY) SCHWAB

Centre for Aboriginal Economic Policy Research
Research School of Social Sciences
College of Arts and Social Sciences
The Australian National University

Australian
National
University

E PRESS

ANU
E PRESS

Published by ANU E Press
The Australian National University
Canberra ACT 0200, Australia
Email: anuepress@anu.edu.au
This title is also available online at http://epress.anu.edu.au

---

National Library of Australia Cataloguing-in-Publication entry

Author: Kral, Inge.

Title: Learning spaces : youth, literacy and new media in remote Indigenous Australia /
                Inge Kral and Robert G. Schwab.

ISBN: 9781922144089 (pbk.) 9781922144096 (ebook)

Notes: Includes bibliographical references and index.

Subjects: Computers and literacy--Australia.
                Aboriginal Australians--Effect of technological innovations on.
                Learning--Technological innovations--Australia.

Other Authors/Contributors:
                Schwab, Robert G.

Dewey Number: 371.26

Design by Gillian Cosgrove.

Front cover photograph by Alan Nash, 2012, © Ngaanyatjarra Media.

This edition © 2012 ANU E Press

Contents

Contents CONTINUED

List of images

List of images CONTINUED

Acknowledgements

This research project was made possible through joint funding from the Australian Research Council, The Australian National University and The Fred Hollows Foundation. We also wish to acknowledge the enormous in-kind contribution of all the individuals and organisations involved in this project, many of whom played multiple roles in collaborating in the research and/or providing technical and production input, ideas and inspiration:

ALICE SPRINGS PUBLIC LIBRARY
Fiona Blackburn

AUSTRALIAN NATIONAL UNIVERSITY
Paul Maclay – ANU Multimedia Services (Video Production)

AUSTRALIAN NATIONAL UNIVERSITY – CENTRE FOR ABORIGINAL ECONOMIC POLICY RESEARCH
Gillian Cosgrove, Martin Heskins, John Hughes, Frances Morphy, Sumathi Renganathan, Denise Steele

BATCHELOR INSTITUTE FOR INDIGENOUS TERTIARY EDUCATION
Margaret Carew

CENTRAL LAND COUNCIL
Jane Hodson

DJILPIN ARTS
Susan Ashley, Rebecca Cooper, Chantelle Doctor, Augustina Kennedy, Ani Lewis, Tom E. Lewis, Sasha Lindsay, Anna McLeod, Fleur Parry, Amos Urban, Ricardo Weston
Photos: © Djilpin Arts

INDIGENOUS YOUTH LEADERSHIP PROGRAM
Joe Ross

JAWOYN ASSOCIATION
Wes Miller

LAJAMANU COMMUNITY
Steve Patrick, Maxwell Tasman, Shane White

MEDIA TRAINERS AND PRODUCERS
Anna Cadden, Ben Foley

NGAANYATJARRA MEDIA
Nathan Brown, Belle Davidson, Delwyn Davidson, Daniel Featherstone, John Gordon, Marcia Mitchell, Anthony Nelson, Natalie O'Toole, Monty O'Toole, Chris Reid, Noelie Roberts, Nina Tsernjavski, Alunytjuru Band from Wingellina, Sunset Reggae Band from Kalka
Photos: © Ngaanyatjarra Media/Valerie Bichard/ Alan Nash

NGAPARTJI NGAPARTJI
Belinda Abbott, Joanne Andrews, Trevor Jamieson, Alex Kelly, Jane Leonard, Julie Miller, Dani Powell, Sadie Richards, Beth Sometimes, Maureen Watson, Elton Wirri
Photos: © Ngapartji Ngapartji/Keith Saunders

NORTHERN TERRITORY LIBRARY
Jason Gibson, Jo McGill, Cate Richmond

PAW MEDIA AND COMMUNICATIONS

STANFORD UNIVERSITY, USA
Shirley Brice Heath

THE FRED HOLLOWS FOUNDATION
Gemina Corpus, Deb Dank, Brian Doolan,
Alison Edwards, Betty Hounslow, Shellie Morris

TI TREE COMMUNITY
Gayle Campbell, Lana Campbell, James Glenn,
Marcia Long

**UNIVERSITY OF CALIFORNIA
LOS ANGELES, USA**
Eve Tulbert

UNIVERSITY OF NEW SOUTH WALES
Martin Nakata

**WARBURTON YOUTH ARTS PROJECT
(NOW WILURARRA CREATIVE)**

WARLPIRI EDUCATION AND TRAINING TRUST
Danielle Campbell, Georgie Stewart

**WARLPIRI YOUTH DEVELOPMENT
ABORIGINAL CORPORATION**
Francis Forrest, Amy Hardy, Kyle Jarvie,
Sue Lovett, Susie Low, Azaria Robertson, Kate
Webb, Micah Wenitong

Further acknowledgements

Stills from the *Stories in Land* Film Project used
with permission from Ninti One Ltd. *Stories
in Land* was a CSIRO RIRDC funded Project,
undertaken as part of the Desert Knowledge Co-
operative Research Centre (DKCRC) Livelihoods
in Land project/Core Project 1 in partnership with
PAW Media and Communications.

Anmatyerr language materials prepared in
conjunction with 'Certificate II in Own Language
Work' students at the Centre for Australian
languages and Linguistics, Batchelor Institute
for Indigenous Tertiary Education (BIITE),
Alice Springs.

A special thank you to Margaret Carew,
Daniel Featherstone and Frances Morphy for
their valuable comments on early drafts.

Abbreviations and acronyms

AIATSIS	Australian Institute of Aboriginal and Torres Islander Studies
ANU	Australian National University
APY	Anangu Pitjantjatjara Yankunytjatjara
ARC	Australian Research Council
BIITE	Batchelor Institute of Indigenous Tertiary Education
BRACS	Broadcasting in Remote Aboriginal Communities Scheme
CAAMA	Central Australian Aboriginal Media Association
CDU	Charles Darwin University
DET	Department of Education (NT)
DKCRC	Desert Knowledge Co-operative Research Centre
FHF	The Fred Hollows Foundation
ICT	Information and Communication Technology
ICTV	Indigenous Community Television
ITIC	Information Technology and Indigenous Communities
LKC	Library and Knowledge Centre
NAPLAN	National Assessment Program – Literacy and Numeracy
NITV	National Indigenous Television
NPY	Ngaanyatjarra Pitjantjatjara Yankunytjatjara
NT	Northern Territory
NTFO	Northern Territory Film Office
NTL	Northern Territory Library
PAW Media	Pintupi Anmatjere Warlpiri Media
RIMO	Remote Indigenous Media Organisation
SAE	Standard Australian English
TEABBA	Top End Aboriginal Bush Broadcasting Association
VET	Vocational Education and Training
WA	Western Australia
WETT	Warlpiri Education and Training Trust

Aboriginal language words

anangu	Aboriginal person (Pitjantjatjara language)
kartiya	non-Aboriginal person/whitefella (Warlpiri language)
ngapartji-ngapartji	reciprocity, 'I give you something in return' (Pitjantjatjara language)
yapa	Aboriginal person (Warlpiri language)

Foreword

SHIRLEY BRICE HEATH

An anthropological linguist, Professor Shirley Brice Heath has spent more than three decades studying how and when young people learn the future anew. She has recorded the ways they survey, critique, adapt, complement, and alter the learning environments around them. She has documented from her time spent, year after year, with young people, who feel intensely that schooling and its limited perspectives on literacy and numeracy do not match the rapid pace of change. As a consequence, young people around the world find ways outside of schooling to create their own opportunities to experiment and innovate with new technologies. They devise entrepreneurial ventures to promote their learning and integrate literacies of all types from visual to financial into their ways of interacting. Since 1980, she has been a frequent colleague of anthropologists, linguists, and educators in universities across Australia. In the United States, she has worked closely with researchers who are exploring the changing learning contexts of adolescents and Indigenous populations.

We live in an era of innovations and cutting edges. Changes come too rapidly to be noted by those of us who do not live with them on a daily basis. We may ask whether or not it matters that the world does not see or take note of the ways that habits of communication shift, while governments and age-old institutions, such as education, remain relatively unchanged in their patterns of operation or their expectations that their beliefs and means need not change.

Where are the adaptations and adoptions taking place, and why do they draw international attention? Adopters and adapters are young people, from those who find the national brand of education their government offers inadequate to their needs to those who go along with the norms of schooling and see certificates and diplomas as building blocks toward employment.

Learning Spaces offers us the rare opportunity to step inside innovative uses of technologies, mergers of global technologies into local knowledge, and community advocacy of local history and ideology. This work joins the volumes of research that point to the limited goals and means of schooling and illustrate the vitality of young people's desire to be challenged to build knowledge and skills for the future and to escape the boredom and inertia of textbooks, lessons, and passive classrooms. Readers will find within the wide range of examples illustrated here in detail models of ways to meet the twin goals of keeping Aboriginal youth in school and simultaneously taking advantage of their leadership toward change.

This volume reminds us that envisioning change primarily through formal education will increasingly limit human potential. Institutions have across human history developed in order to maintain the status quo; hence, they have within them inherent protections against change that may come so rapidly as to overthrow or dislodge the power and predictability they present. However, in times of rapid technological change that reaches into the most intimate aspects of human relations and socialization, change in ways of learning must come. These ways honour and instantiate some of the oldest and most trustworthy capacities of humans: attentive and sustained listening and observing, working out new ways through trial and error, and adapting both technologies themselves and ways of using them.

The lessons from this volume relate most directly to the nature of learning within communities and organisations. These entities, unlike institutions, have been created throughout human history in order to provide adaptability and flexibility for change. They are built in and through change, and within them, change has astonishing promise.

The cases within this volume call on us to observe, listen, imitate, and create from the cases of change documented here. Doing so promises innovation and inspiration. Even more important, these cases help all of us keep in mind the humanity and the human that learning by creating provides. The young people who move through these pages are motivated and proud of having had the opportunities that make possible their linking together of historical knowledge and contemporary means of communication and performance. The means illustrated here have enabled them to develop skills that will help them move into the future as adults engaged with the health and life of their own communities, connected to their language and culture as their way of being in the world of the local so as to know the world of the global.

SHIRLEY BRICE HEATH
Stanford University
California USA

CHAPTER 1

INTRODUCTION

The future of Indigenous Australians, especially Indigenous youth, in remote regions is a subject of great concern to all Australians. The view commonly presented in media reports and public commentary is unrelentingly bleak. While we recognise the challenges young people face, in this book we intend to dispute that view. The prevalent media images, newspaper headlines and opinion pages are so focused on examples of dysfunction that few Australians would ever imagine that many Indigenous young people are quietly leading productive and meaningful lives and moving confidently toward a future while walking in two worlds. Throughout this book you will meet some of these Indigenous young and dedicated individuals who reinvigorate faith in the potential that lies unacknowledged in the remote context. Our aim is to showcase a range of 'out-of-school' youth learning contexts in remote Australia, to analyse the factors that enable positive learning and to provide some working principles for facilitating and supporting effective youth learning in the remote Indigenous context.

THE RESEARCH PROJECT

In 2007 we—Inge Kral and Jerry Schwab— embarked on an ethnographic research project in partnership with The Fred Hollows Foundation and The Northern Territory Library. Then, as now, low school attendance, poor English literacy scores and the educational and social disengagement of young people in remote Indigenous communities was portrayed as a 'crisis'. While we acknowledge that mainstream education is an effective learning pathway for some, our combined experience in working with Indigenous communities in remote Australia suggested that there were many Indigenous young people in those communities for whom mainstream education appeared not to hold the answers to their visions of the future. Consequently, we were keen to explore other pathways to learning and other options for re-engaging the young people who find themselves outside the fence of institutional learning. Specifically, we decided we would not explore the merit or otherwise of education 'in school'. Rather, our research focuses on two domains: ongoing learning in the out-of-school hours, and ongoing learning across the lifespan. Accordingly, our interest is in two groups: early school-leavers (aged sixteen and above) and young adults in the post-school age group. Our project, the *Lifespan Learning and Literacy for Young Adults in Remote Indigenous Communities* project, asks three key questions:

▶ how can early school leavers and disaffected young adults in remote communities be re-engaged with learning;

▶ how can literacy be acquired, maintained and transmitted outside school settings; and

▶ how can learning and literacy be fostered across the lifespan?

The *Lifespan Learning and Literacy for Young Adults in Remote Indigenous Communities* (2007–2010), later known as the 'Youth Learning Project', was jointly funded by the Australian Research Council (ARC), The Australian National University (ANU) and The Fred Hollows Foundation (FHF). This participatory research project explored, documented and showcased the many ways in which Indigenous youth—aged between 16 and 25—are extending their learning, expanding their oral and written language skills, and embracing digital culture in community-based domains outside of institutional learning environments. Jerry Schwab was the project's Chief Investigator and Inge Kral was an ARC Postdoctoral Fellow. Professor Emerita Shirley Brice Heath from Stanford University in the United States was an important collaborator and advisor to the project. Though focused broadly across a range of communities and organisations, an important feature of the project was the close collaboration that evolved between the researchers and around fifteen young people and organisation facilitators from key research sites in the Northern Territory and Western Australia:

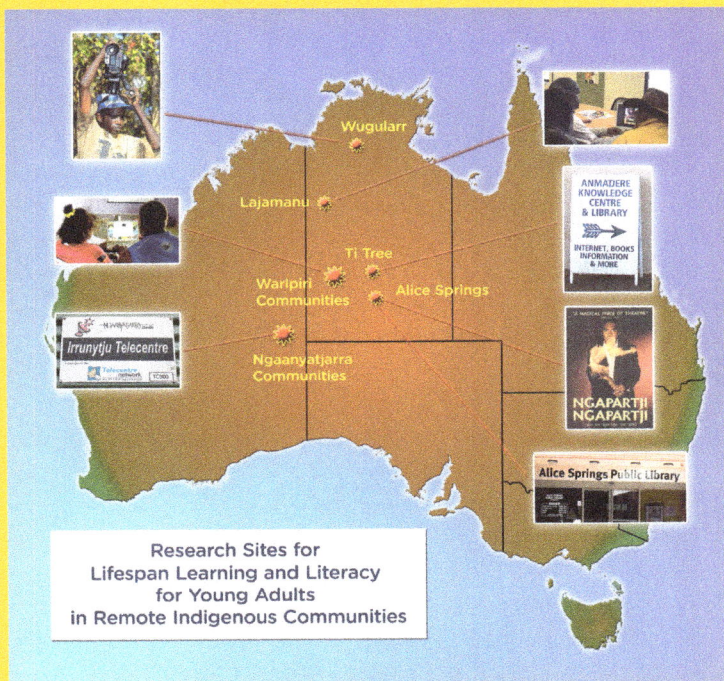

Research Sites for
Lifespan Learning and Literacy
for Young Adults
in Remote Indigenous Communities

NGAANYATJARRA MEDIA, at Wingellina in Western Australia

LIBRARIES AND KNOWLEDGE CENTRES at Lajamanu and Ti Tree in the Northern Territory

DJILPIN ARTS ABORIGINAL CORPORATION at Beswick (Wugularr) in the Northern Territory

YOUTH PROGRAMS at Yuendumu, Nyirripi, Willowra and Lajamanu in the Northern Territory

NGAPARTJI NGAPARTJI intergenerational language and arts project in Alice Springs in the Northern Territory

THE ALICE SPRINGS PUBLIC LIBRARY in the Northern Territory

As the project got underway it quickly became clear that a key feature of literacy and learning among Indigenous youth in remote Australia today is their adoption of and intense engagement with digital media. This new reality reframed our original research questions and has given our project—and this book—its particular focus.

In our research we noticed that although many young people may be walking away from compulsory schooling and training, they are not rejecting *learning*. Instead, and importantly, our observations and interactions with young people indicate that when alternative learning opportunities are provided, youth are participating and successful outcomes are being attained. Our research shows that through engagement in locally-based, personally meaningful projects, youth are forming the understandings, skills and competencies they require to enter young adulthood as bilingual, bicultural beings—drawing on the language and culture transmitted by their elders, but also transforming it. They are also developing the linguistic and conceptual tools—and the work-oriented habits and attitudes—required to move towards responsible adult roles. Significantly, many are doing this in learning environments that are outside school or post-school training and so remain invisible to many policy-makers and government officials. These learning environments, or *learning spaces* as we call them and elaborate in detail later, effectively stimulate productive learning and the acquisition and development of language and multimodal literacies, organisational learning, enterprise generation and employment. Here young people (even those with minimal education) are developing the agency and creative capacity to determine new pathways that differ from previous generations.

In this book we seek to portray the creativity and agentive participation of remote Indigenous youth. In particular we explore their involvement with their communities and the outside world, and with organisations and sites that catalyse learning and engagement. We show them to be deeply committed to learning; able to speak, and often literate in, one or more languages; fluent in new forms of cultural practice and production; and active participants in the changing modes of communication in the digital age.

The aim of our project was not to find a replicable or prescriptive model or method but to look at the factors that create the learning spaces that support productive activities. Drawing on what we have observed from the various individuals, communities and organisations, our research seeks to promote approaches that successfully re-engage young adults with ongoing learning and literacy development outside school and formal training. Although the contexts that we present differ, some principles are transferable. It is those principles, detailed in a later chapter, which we believe can support sustainable language and literacy development, learning and cultural production.

THE RESEARCH JOURNEY

We approached this research project with a large degree of scepticism about current approaches to literacy and schooling in the remote Indigenous context. Having seen many new education policy initiatives and curriculum innovations come and go with little apparent long-term change, we were interested in exploring non-institutional approaches to youth, learning and literacy that have been detailed in the international literature, yet remain largely unexplored in remote Australia. As we will show later, that literature resonated strongly with our individual experiences in many remote Indigenous communities. Significantly, much of the emerging international literature attempts to move beyond conventional theories of learning focused on schooling. This literature emphasises a socio-cultural theory of learning and a view of literacy as social practice. Moreover, it indicates that assumptions about how and where learning should take place are being challenged by new youth media practices.

Importantly, we approached the research as anthropologists rather than educationalists. As researchers we brought different perspectives to the project. Jerry is an anthropologist specialising in education with many years of research experience working with Indigenous people in Australia and overseas. Inge is a linguistic anthropologist who has spent more than two decades working in the field of Indigenous language and literacy in remote Australia as an educator and researcher. As a discipline, anthropology—and its key methodology of ethnography—offers a unique and powerful lens for exploring issues of learning, youth, media and literacy.

Why anthropology?

Our ethnographic approach is underpinned by theory from anthropology. Anthropology as an academic discipline encompasses many fields. Notably, literacy has been a key object of study in anthropology. Over recent decades studies in education anthropology, linguistic anthropology and sociolinguistics have shifted the emphasis away from a traditional, cognitivist view of literacy as a set of technical skills that are possessed or lacked, towards studies of the social and cultural behaviour associated with literacy. A fundamental tenet of anthropology is that cultural forms are transmitted from one generation to the next through socialisation, as well as direct and indirect teaching and learning. In this study, we wanted to examine how learners acquire (or are socialised into) the dispositions, knowledge, skills and practices (including language and literacy) required to function as competent members of social groups and cultural communities, in out-of-school settings.

Why ethnography?

Linguists and anthropologists have opened up new understandings of the interrelationship between culture and literacy with the application of ethnographic methods to the study of communication. Ethnographic studies of literacy stand at the interface between anthropology and sociolinguistics and look at the social practices, social meanings, and the cultural conceptions of reading and writing. As researchers we have been strongly influenced by anthropologists Brian Street and Shirley Brice Heath and their ethnographic approaches to language and literacy research (Heath 1983; Heath and Street 2008; Street 1995). Street and Heath suggest that an ethnographic approach requires researchers to take young people and their cultural practices seriously by looking at what *is* happening, rather than what is *not* happening. Consequently, the ethnographic approach undertaken in our project emphasised detailed descriptions and portrayals of what is happening on the ground in specific communities. That ethnography provided the raw material from which we drew insights into various developmental pathways for youth. Importantly, one of the outcomes of the ethnographic approach was a resultant shift in the focus away from a deficit perspective, to highlighting the positive manner in which Indigenous youth are interpreting and responding to contemporary circumstances with creative agency.

Typically, ethnographic methods include:

▶ participant observation (observing while being involved as a participant in the everyday activities of the people involved in the study);

▶ writing field notes about what happens;

▶ making audio-visual recordings of events and activities;

▶ gathering contextually relevant artefacts; and

▶ conducting formal and informal interviews with people involved with the study.

In this project we used a participatory or collaborative ethnographic research methodology to investigate the ways in which Indigenous youth are extending their learning and expanding their language and multimodal literacy practices through engaging with digital technologies and multimedia production.

Ethnographic 'data' was gathered in projects and sites from participant observation, ethnographic notes and in-depth interviews to build locally informed accounts of the social processes shaping youth learning, language and literacy practices.

Additional data informed our understanding about what was happening on the ground:

▶ Limited collection of base-line data on post-school age adults including: education, training and employment background; and measures of language, literacy and numeracy competence.

▶ The collection and documentation of perceptions of opportunities and options for the development of community learning and literacy in non-school contexts.

▶ The observation and analysis of youth cultural productions (films, songs, theatre) and audio-visual recordings of language use and practice in learning, production and performance.

Finally, a review of existing literature filtered connections and observations through various theoretical frameworks.

Why youth?

While enormous research effort has gone into the study of Indigenous children in school, in part because research in institutional settings is easier, research in 'out-of-school' settings or among youth who have left school is relatively rare. The latter is true, we believe, because media and government policies typically view many young people in remote Indigenous communities as a 'lost generation', illiterate, unemployed and drifting. Yet our experience suggested this was not necessarily the case and so we set out to explore more deeply the reality of life and learning among these young people.

Though ethnographic accounts of contemporary youth practice are few and seldom privilege the youth voice (Hirschfeld 2002), anthropology is 'well-situated' to offer an account of how youth in different socio-cultural contexts 'produce and negotiate cultural forms' (Bucholtz 2002: 526). In Australia few anthropologists work directly with adolescents or young adults in remote Indigenous contexts and few accounts reflect the actual practices and perspectives of young people. In fact, Indigenous youth have been relatively invisible or marginal to anthropological research altogether. While a handful of ethnographies or anthropological studies refer to children and adolescents, primarily within classical life cycle descriptions (for example, Malinowski 1963; Goodale 1971; Tonkinson 1978), few have specifically focused on children or youth. Annette Hamilton's important study of child rearing in Arnhem Land (Hamilton 1981) and Victoria Burbank's account of female adolescence in an Aboriginal community

(Burbank 1988) are two exceptions. More recently, ethnographic accounts have focused on the negative consequences of rapid socio-cultural change (Brady 1992; Robinson 1990), while others have addressed complex issues associated with changing youth socialisation (Fietz 2008), learning (Fogarty 2010), and intergenerational change (Eickelkamp 2011). Nevertheless, there are immense gaps in our knowledge of contemporary adolescence and little attention has been paid to critical questions associated with adolescent development, learning, language socialisation, and cultural production and transmission. Yet internationally, as we discuss further later, a growing body of ethnographic research is addressing adolescent language socialisation, learning and new media in community-based settings.

Why digital media?

As mentioned earlier, what began as an ethnographic research project oriented around youth learning and the acquisition and use of alphabetic literacy practices in everyday settings dramatically altered over the course of the project in response to the real world context that we were encountering. What we discovered was that we were observing and documenting a broad spectrum of changing youth practice in the remote Indigenous world, much of which was starting to pivot around digital media. As time went on it became apparent that our research was uncovering local examples of the profound changes in communication practices worldwide brought about by the onset of the digital revolution and the associated impact on social, cultural and technological practices and

Indigenous teachers and the growing emphasis on nationally standardised English language National Assessment Program—Literacy and Numeracy (NAPLAN) benchmark testing. All of these have contributed to undermining the potential of the process of formal schooling in remote Indigenous Australia. The NAPLAN tests deployed in remote schools almost invariably show that Indigenous students lag well behind other students in terms of their literacy, numeracy, writing and other skills as measured by such tests. We would argue that standardised tests are blunt instruments for assessing the capacities of students; they are problematic in that they actually tell us little about students' capacities for learning or how to most effectively support learning either inside or outside the classroom (Schwab 2012). Nonetheless, NAPLAN test results are used uncritically by the media and politicians as a shorthand method of gauging and comparing educational outcomes. In Indigenous communities and schools, media attention has been harsh and the refrain of 'failure' has been relentless. It is perhaps not surprising that early school leavers (most of whom have disengaged from formal learning) comprise the majority of young people in remote Indigenous communities.

While we certainly need to reconsider the 'schooling' of Indigenous youth, we also need to pay much more attention to the process of ongoing and adaptive learning across the lifespan that goes on outside school. Similarly, we need to highlight the important role played by youth-oriented organisations in facilitating many aspects of youth learning. It is these points that we elaborate in this book.

processes. Indeed, over the past decade youth and digital media have become the subject of substantial ethnographic inquiry (Buckingham 2008b; Hull 2003; Ito et al. 2010) generating a wave of interest in changing communication modes and learning processes.[1]

Why learning?

Readers may wonder why we focus on 'learning' rather than 'education' or 'schooling'? Over the years we have witnessed the sincere efforts of many hard-working and inspired professional educators and we in no way wish to diminish their accomplishments. What is apparent however is that no matter how committed teachers are to educating Indigenous youth, the issues are increasingly complex and require solutions beyond the traditional calls for the provision of better resourced schools and better trained teachers. The situation has not been assisted by the dismantling of good bilingual programs, the marginalisation of local

Our research on the ways Indigenous young people engage and re-engage with learning begins with a purposeful step away from traditional educational notions of knowledge acquisition as a formal instructional process deliverable in bite-size chunks to waiting students. In this traditional model, knowledge is 'taught'. It is decontextualised and abstracted from everyday life: content is separate from context. By contrast, our research has been deeply informed by the notion of 'situated learning' and its emphasis on context, 'social practice', and engagement in learning at all stages of life through both formal and informal means.

We posit that learning is a fundamental feature of human life. It can take place through three different mechanisms (Gee 2004: 11-13). First, learning may involve a natural, seemingly unconscious process—for example in acquiring a first language or learning to walk. In contrast, learning may take place through overt instruction; learning physics or calculus, for example, requires explicit instruction. In this second form of learning it quickly becomes clear that not everyone has the same capacity to learn and understand the principles and application of specific bodies of knowledge. A third learning process can be described as cultural, where learners observe masters at work over an extended period of time. In this process masters model techniques or behaviours and the learners imitate (and often fail). Ultimately the learners 'learn by doing' and gain competence and earn a new identity, as a mechanic or a chef, for example.

In our research we found that learning that was most effectively stimulated and fostered in particular contexts or sites was of the third type. These sites we characterise as 'productive': as sites where learning involves the production of new knowledge, skills, confidence and often the reconfiguration of identity. These sites we have called *learning spaces*. Our description and analysis of productive learning in these sites is the focus of this book.

HOW THE PROJECT EVOLVED

As we have established, in this project we have used an ethnographic approach to language and literacy research. Ethnographic accounts of remote Indigenous youth tend to be acquired only when researchers can develop long-term associations and immerse themselves in a collaborative endeavour where trust and relationships are slowly developed.

As the primary researcher on the ground, Inge visited each of the main research sites for differing amounts of time throughout 2007 and 2008. She met many young people and community and program facilitators and used standard participant observation methodology and open-ended interview techniques, as well as gathering baseline literacy data. It was at this point that it became clear that digital media had become integral to young people's everyday social and cultural practice and was an important dynamic in the ethnographic research process. In March 2009 fifteen young people and facilitators from six of the sites were brought together for a week-long workshop at Thakeperte, an outstation near Alice Springs. At this workshop a compilation DVD of the young people's work and digital stories was made. Out of this workshop emerged a core group of youth research collaborators (who you see named on pages 12–13 and whose quotes appear throughout this volume). By meeting each other and sharing and producing media work together they started to identify with each other as a group and a reciprocal learning and research relationship developed. In 2008 and 2010 we presented our preliminary research findings at the American Anthropological Association Annual meeting and met with colleagues Shirley Brice Heath and Glynda Hull. Inge also visited similar community based youth organisations in the United States.[2] These interactions confirmed that we were on the right track.

Inge made a further fieldwork visit to each of the sites in mid 2009 and collected an additional set of audio-visual recordings. This visit consolidated the growing relationship of trust and mutual respect. It also led to two of the key youth participants, Shane White and Maxwell Tasman from Lajamanu Community, travelling to Darwin with Inge to present their work and the outcomes of the research project at the *Symposium on Indigenous Dance and Music* at Charles Darwin University (CDU) in August 2009.[3] A month later, in September 2009, ten young people and their project facilitators came together for a three day workshop at the ANU's North Australia Research Unit campus in Darwin. During this workshop we filmed and edited four short films and prepared oral presentations for our one day public *Youth Learning Symposium* at the Darwin Convention Centre with an invited group of over a hundred academics, researchers, policymakers and those who work directly with youth organisations.[4]

As ethnographers in this project our job has been to notice what others often don't notice about young people. In other words, by taking young people and their activities seriously the focus can be shifted away from a deficit perspective on youth learning and cultural practice, to highlighting the positive manner in which Indigenous youth are interpreting and responding to contemporary circumstances with creative agency. Though not our goal, in many ways our research findings are unarguably an affirmation of Indigenous youth potential. In working alongside young people in a collaborative manner, we gained insights into the capacity of youth, the meanings they attach to definitions of success, and their enacted intentions to shape their social surroundings and future options.

Importantly, the young people in this research project have had agency in the research process and in their own self-representation. Furthermore, through involvement in the project they have become aware that their various projects, productions and ideas have value not only in their own community, but also to a national, and international, audience.

YOUTH
LEARNING
SYMPOSIUM,
DARWIN 2009
PHOTO: YOUTH
LEARNING
PROJECT

While many of the young people we observed and who taught us about themselves and their lives seem remarkable, they are not necessarily atypical. Many have found school alienating, training programs frustrating and unfulfilling and they have struggled to find their own way to contribute and grow toward adult responsibilities in their home communities. Many were early school leavers and would be assessed as having low English literacy skills yet they have blossomed when they have found local, creative activities that have value to them and their communities. They are 'below the radar', quietly doing meaningful work (though not always recognised as such). Interestingly many did not think of themselves as particularly special or different from other Indigenous young people in terms of capacity, but they saw themselves as responsible and committed to purposeful, productive activity.

Though we never envisaged it as such, the ethnographic process itself has been transformative, acting as a catalyst and enabling young people to begin a dialogue with researchers and others from outside their world, to stand outside their everyday context. They have begun to participate in public domains and debates, as evidenced in the growing presence of youth media workers at national conferences and symposia.[5] In our view this highlights the need for other researchers to work directly with adolescents or young adults in remote contexts, and to provide accounts that reflect the actual practices and perspectives of Indigenous youth (Kral 2011b). Such an approach mirrors the international trend towards the development of collaborative approaches to youth research (Cammarota 2008; Heath and Street 2008; Jessor et al. 1996; McCarty and Wyman 2009) and research in minority Indigenous contexts (Fluehr-Lobban 2008).

KEY YOUTH PARTICIPANTS AND COLLABORATORS

AMOS URBAN

AUGUSTINA KENNEDY

AZARIA ROBERTSON

BELINDA O'TOOLE

CHRIS REID

ELTON WIRRI

JOANNE ANDREWS

FRANCIS FORREST

GAYLE CAMPBELL

JULIE MILLER

LANA CAMPBELL

MAUREEN WATSON

MAXWELL TASMAN

NATALIE O'TOOLE

NATHAN BROWN

REVONNA URBAN

RICARDO WESTON

SADIE WILLIAMS

SHANE WHITE

I really enjoyed doing the Youth Learning research. I've learned a lot of good things and meeting other young people from different communities. It was important to do this research because we know that we can do all these things. If we learn a little bit then we can get started. It's important to let the people know that we can do all these things, not just whitefellas, but other young people, by encouraging them.

To me doing this research has changed a lot how I think about things. Now that I have shown the white people that I can do this and that. So that in the future if the community needs help I would know what to do, how to help them. So come and work with us and we'll show you what we can do. Working together as a team, like *ngapartji-ngapartji* and learning about each other for the future. We'll show you what we can do and how we want to do it. It's like a kick-start for all young people like us. It's really important for the younger generation, for how they are gonna grow up and how they are gonna be: finding the balance *anangu* way and whitefella way.

NATALIE O'TOOLE
WINGELLINA COMMUNITY, 2010

With this research thing we learnt new ideas from different people from different communities and we can share our skills with each other and we can make it useful. By meeting all the different people from other places, by all the groups working together we started to understand different things. When we first started doing the research it all changed, like we went to different places and met other people, with their skills and ideas and like putting all those things altogether and using it. Like we'll have it on a DVD or book so that people can look at it... So all the different things that we been learning, that's for people to look at it and understand how we been learning.

So from this research thing, that's where all the ideas and skills like come altogether in one, you know. So people can use these ideas, like young people, younger generation can look at these sort of things that we been doing and all the other different communities are doing, all the activities, and anything. Music, all those things. And now, to us, we see it as, like it all comes all in one, as one big idea, you know. Lots of ideas in one. Like that, for people to look at and to use in the future...

CHRIS REID
WINGELLINA COMMUNITY, 2010

AIM OF THE BOOK

We admit we are ambitious in our desire that this book should be useful to several audiences. We began the project with a plan to write a community handbook, with a range of practical suggestions and examples to promote literacy and learning. But as the project progressed and we paid more intent attention to what we were observing and learning, it was clear that there was something much more significant emerging than a set of 'best practices'. What we saw was that the Indigenous young people we met and who shared with us their insights and experiences were quietly yet deeply involved in a range of meaningful and productive learning activities in their home communities. At the same time, many were clearly part of an international, and generational, change among youth facilitated by new media. To truly understand what we were seeing, we needed to engage much more deeply with the international conversation and theoretical literature that has up to now had little connection with the remote Indigenous Australian world. The result is a book that we hope will inspire and suggest ideas to communities, but which goes well beyond that original vision of a handbook. We believe this book will have value not only to Indigenous community members but also to youth workers, government officers, policy makers, students, educators and academic colleagues.

In spite of our ambitions, we are well aware that individual readers will find different sections more engaging than others depending on their interests, roles and experiences. For example, the case studies will assist readers who want to know 'what' or 'how' while the theoretical sections will assist readers who want to understand 'why'. Though we have aimed for a layout that is readable, engaging and accessible, inviting readers to dip in and out of various sections, we believe that the individual chapters do provide a range of connected stories. These stories portray the often rich lives of many young people in many remote communities—their experiences of learning, literacy, new media and their pathways through life and work. We hope *Learning Spaces* will provide policy makers with a new perspective on Indigenous youth in remote communities, as well as insights and ideas about how future policy might be shaped. At the same time, we believe the descriptions of various learning spaces and the productive learning occurring within them will inspire youth workers and Indigenous community members to think creatively about how to support formal, and informal, learning in their communities.

STRUCTURE OF THIS BOOK

In this chapter we have provided an introduction to the project from which the book emerged. We have set out our research questions and approach, our methods and our disciplinary backgrounds. We have also sketched the key theories that underpin our view of what we observed and learned. In all this we have tried to set the stage for the book and attempted to lead the reader through the logic of our research, explaining how, where and why we have focused on youth, learning and new media. In Chapter 2 we develop the ideas of *learning spaces* and 'productive learning' and provide an overview of the sites and settings within which we worked. Chapter 3 is more theoretical than the other chapters and moves the discussion from the local to the global by connecting elements of learning spaces and productive learning described in Chapter 2 with international research through a focused series of questions related to literacy, learning, media, youth and identity. In Chapter 4 we draw on more examples from our research and build on insights from international theory and research to provide a series of design principles for learning spaces in remote Australia. Chapter 5 summarises the main findings of our research and suggests what we believe are the most important implications for communities, practitioners and policy makers.

Chapter 1 endnotes

1. Australian researchers have also addressed youth issues (Wyn et al. 2005) and media technologies in remote Indigenous settings (Dyson et al. 2007; Ormond-Parker et al. 2012; Rennie et al. 2010).

2. Visits were made to Artists for Humanity in Boston MA: http://www.afhboston.com/ and Riverzedge Arts Project in Woonsocket RI: http://riverzedgearts.org/

3. 8th Annual Symposium on Indigenous Dance and Music for the National Recording Project for Indigenous Performance in Australia, Charles Darwin University, Darwin, August 15 2009.

4. At the Youth Learning Symposium connections were made with Eve Tulbert, an anthropology graduate student from the University of California, Los Angeles and Nora Kenney from the Kidnet research project connecting adolescent youth aged 12–18 around the world via a private social network (Space2Cre8: http://www.space2cre8.com).

5. For example the Australian Institute of Aboriginal and Torres Strait Islander Studies (AIATSIS) 2010 Information Technology and Indigenous Communities (ITIC) Symposium, Canberra 2010 and the AIATSIS National Indigenous Studies Conference, Canberra 2011.

CHAPTER 2

THE LEARNING SPACES

In this chapter we introduce the research sites by elaborating on two concepts we consider elemental in our research. First, we consider the idea of *learning spaces*, and second, the nature of the 'productive learning' that these spaces generate.

In Australia today, public and policy discourse promotes schooling and vocational training as the primary pathway to realising successful futures for remote Indigenous youth. However this ideal model appears to have little resonance in many communities where there are few job opportunities and a considerable number of young people are voting with their feet by walking away from institutional learning. This is distressing not only to educators and politicians, but also to many Indigenous families who are continually told, and firmly believe, that 'school' should provide the knowledge and tools—including English literacy and numeracy—necessary for economic participation and success and the transition to adult life. To

understand why Indigenous youth disengage from education it is important to explore the degree to which their schooling experience has relevance to the social and cultural realities of their lives.

Some of what is seen as the withdrawal of Indigenous youth from formal education and training may in fact be the agency of youth in expressions of resistance and identity (Bottrell 2007) or 'self-sabotage' resulting from the experience of discrimination and racism (Andrews et al. 2008). Together these may account for much of what might be observed not so much as 'failure' but rather as a 'retreat from aspiration' among young people (Bottrell 2007: 610). At the same time it is important to acknowledge that in remote Indigenous contexts, mainstream credentialing is not necessarily perceived as a prerequisite for a fulfilling life. In fact, in the communities we worked with, other socio-cultural schemas continue to firmly underpin the practice of everyday life and the construction of social identity. The obligations to culture, country and kin remain primary while formal education and its promised rewards of employment are secondary. Given the relatively small amount of time that even the most dedicated Indigenous young people spend in formal learning on any one day and across the life span (Schwab 1999), it is unrealistic to expect schooling alone to deliver the positive identity formation experiences, oral and written communication skills, technological know-how, and the social and organisational learning required to make the transition from adolescence to adulthood. Schools in remote Aboriginal communities (or elsewhere) cannot by themselves 'create' engaged workers and active participants in local and national spheres, especially in locations where families and communities are fragmented

NGAANYATJARRA LANDS ©NGAANYATJARRA MEDIA

and struggling to maintain effective socialisation and learning frameworks.[1]

Our experience and observations in a number of remote communities over decades suggest that there is now not simply a lack of engagement with school but also a learning engagement gap in the out-of-school and post-school years. This is exemplified in one of the research sites where the linkages between school, training and employment are weak and the community has had little social cohesion. An observer describes how many community members had lost hope: 'Young people are often from fragmented families and are struggling to find an identity and a sense of purpose'. As is common in many remote communities, few youth-oriented community resources had been provided: no youth centre, and no sport and recreation centre. In this location the establishment of an effective youth program working with youth at risk and the opening of a community owned cultural centre injected a new sense of optimism and purpose into the community.[2]

Importantly, our research indicates that this learning engagement gap can be filled with productive activity that builds on school learning—or makes up for what was not learned at school—and develops the kind of communication, technological and organisational learning skills required for successful futures for Indigenous youth in the twenty first century. We have characterised these activities as examples of *productive learning* which are facilitated within what we call *learning spaces*. In particular, we have found that young people are attracted

to the learning spaces found in arts projects, youth centres and media organisations. Here participation is not contingent upon prior school competencies or qualification and participants are not compelled by any authority to engage. Rather, participation is voluntary. In these learning spaces young people are choosing to engage in modes of learning that give them the creative freedom to explore and express who they are and what they want to be. Although some communities have sport and recreation activities and even a youth centre, many of these were established to provide diversionary activities to keep youngsters away from substance abuse, drinking or delinquent activity. While some of the programs observed were diversionary, others have emerged and grown out of recognition of the potential of Indigenous young people and their interest in and commitment to music, film, culture, language, community and enterprise.

Internationally, ethnographic research has focused on the potential that youth-focused programs and organisations have to support and stimulate sustained learning, and language and literacy development, especially for marginalised youth (Cushman and Emmons 2002; Eidman-

Aadahl 2002; Heath and McLaughlin 1993; Heath and Smyth 1999; Hull 2003; McLaughlin et al. 1994). In this research literature community-based youth groups and their various activities are seen to offer the 'freedoms of time, space, activity and authority that schools as institutions seldom provide' (Heath and Street 2008: 5). They enable long-term, meaningful engagement with experts or mentors in community based organisations where 'learning is associated with observation and a real (as distinct from realistic) sense of participation with regard to the intensity of observation, willingness to make efforts, and openness to failure' (Heath and Street 2008: 75–76). Importantly, such research suggests that arts-based projects and organisations in particular, offer the opportunity for building information, honing skills, performing in risk laden tasks, expressing a sense of self, and also linking with literacy and language development. Heath describes such programs and projects as 're-generative learning environments', a concept we will return to later (Heath 2007: 5)

This research has direct relevance in remote Indigenous contexts where many adolescents are bypassing institutional learning. In many such communities there is rarely anything meaningful for youth to do in the after-school hours, on weekends and throughout the long school holidays and there is minimal home access to creative tools such as cameras, computers or recording technologies, and sometimes even pens and paper.

In the next section we describe the various youth-oriented community-based projects and organisations that informed our ethnographic research, many of which provide the opportunities described above. These projects facilitate a range of learning spaces. Here young learners have, in most cases, incomplete secondary educations and varying levels of literacy competence in both their Indigenous mother tongue (or vernacular) and English. Yet in these learning spaces young people are learning from Indigenous and non-Indigenous mentors, older relatives and each other. They are also structuring their own learning in environments that encourage individual agency and peer learning. They are taking on meaningful roles and responsibilities and extending and expanding their oral and written communication modes and technological skills. What is transformative in the form of learning that we are talking about here, is that young people encounter adults who believe in them and they see themselves as competent and full of potential.

Importantly all of these sites have, in some way, tapped into digital media. The projects we focus on in this book are representative of the many similar projects that have flourished over recent years in remote Indigenous Australia. Some of these include:

▶ the *Deadly Mob* program (now complete) comprising an internet café and website at the Gap Youth Centre in Alice Springs as well as media training for youth in bush communities with no internet access;

- the *Us Mob* online video project;

- the *Warburton Youth Arts Project* (now known as *Wilurarra Creative);*

- the Ngaanyatjarra Pitjantjatjara Yankunytjatjara (NPY) Women's Council youth project in communities in the Northern Territory, South Australia and Western Australia;

- Tangentyere youth programs including CAYLUS (Central Australian Youth Link Up Service) in Central Australian communities and *Drum Atweme* in Alice Springs;

- the *Irrkelantye Learning Centre* in an Alice Springs town camp;

- *Music Outback* at Ti Tree;

- the *Carclew Youth Arts* program in the Anangu Pitjantjatjara Yankunytjatjara Lands in South Australia;

- the *Mulka Project* at Yirrkala, NT;

- the *Gelengu du Gelenguwurru* new media intergenerational project at Warmun in Western Australia;

- the *Pelican Project* Digital Stories, Hopevale, Qld; and

- the *Martu Media* youth media project at Parnngurr, Western Australia embracing youth involvement in the *Yiwarra Kuju* Canning Stock Route project and exhibition.

Those programs out in the community, I like to call them the invisible programs they are so precious for people out there...without having someone watching over them, it's free to come and to share something...People should really look into it and then see the outcomes. Come out to these places and be part of that, you know and share with these young people, you know, and see the different kind of programs like Deadly Mob or Mt Theo, you know. Please, they should come out you know and just spend a week or three days is good enough so that you can get the whole picture of what is really happening. You know, you'll see plenty of smiling faces, families, kids and the whole community. It will lighten up the atmosphere.

INDIGENOUS YOUTH MENTOR AND MUSICIAN
LAJAMANU, 2008

Young people have been doing it before we came. Dozens of movies had been made at Willowra media training. Always been a bit of a hub for this community...

KYLE JARVIE
YOUTH WORKER,
WILLOWRA YOUTH CENTRE, 2009

The proliferation of these approaches to youth practice is indicative of the change sweeping across remote Indigenous youth culture. See Appendix 1 with links to these and other models.

We will now turn to a description of each of the research sites we worked with before exploring more deeply the notion of productive learning.

THE PROJECT SITES

Djilpin Arts Aboriginal Corporation at Beswick (Wugularr)

Djilpin Arts is a community-owned arts organisation in the community of Beswick, also known as Wugularr, some 90 kilometres from the town of Katherine in the Northern Territory. It produces the annual Walking with Spirits Festival, supports a youth and media training project, and operates an arts retail business at the Ghunmarn Culture Centre—a formerly derelict community house renovated and converted into a bright and attractive gallery and training space.

Djilpin Arts started as a loose collective for artists in the community who had never had the support of a local arts enterprise organisation and its associated infrastructure. The focus for the arts organisation is the maintenance of cultural knowledge systems that are useful to people in the contemporary world.

Djilpin Arts emphasises youth learning, employment and enterprise development as priority areas. There are two aspects to the enterprise venture. First, young women have been trained and are now employed to manage and operate the arts retail business at Ghunmarn Culture Centre. In addition, a café and beauty products enterprise (making soap, lip balm and candles out of natural bush medicines and plants) has been established.

Djilpin Arts has also integrated youth media into their various community arts projects. A non-formal digital learning project has been operating for a number of years for youth to engage with their cultural heritage and learn media skills. Young people are now employed to document community arts and cultural activities.[3]

> We are all the young people working in media and working in the cultural centre. And we'll keep going working here and keeping our community strong and keeping our culture strong.
>
> **REVONNA URBAN**
> BESWICK COMMUNITY, 2009

The Ngapartji Ngapartji intergenerational language and arts project is one of a number of national arts projects undertaken by BIG *h*ART Australia's leading arts and social change company. Based in a temporary demountable building in Alice Springs, the *Ngapartji Ngapartji* project (now complete) began in 2004 and involved community members of all ages in a professional national touring theatre performance (*Ngapartji Ngapartji*) and an online Pitjantjatjara language teaching and preservation project. Underpinning the Ngapartji Ngapartji project was a commitment to language and culture maintenance and the facilitation of youth learning. This included the provision of literacy and learning support for

It was good because they [the young people] found out how to communicate through the arts, through theatre. Theatre has a certain protocol, has also a similar protocol with their traditional ways, their performing and telling stories and such so they understood that...Just keep reminding young people 'you done it, you did this here, you accomplished...and they can walk away proud because they've accomplished something that has changed people's lives...If they keep reminding themselves of that, then they can do anything!'

TREVOR JAMIESON
CO-CREATOR OF THE
NGAPARTJI NGAPARTJI
THEATRE PERFORMANCE, 2008

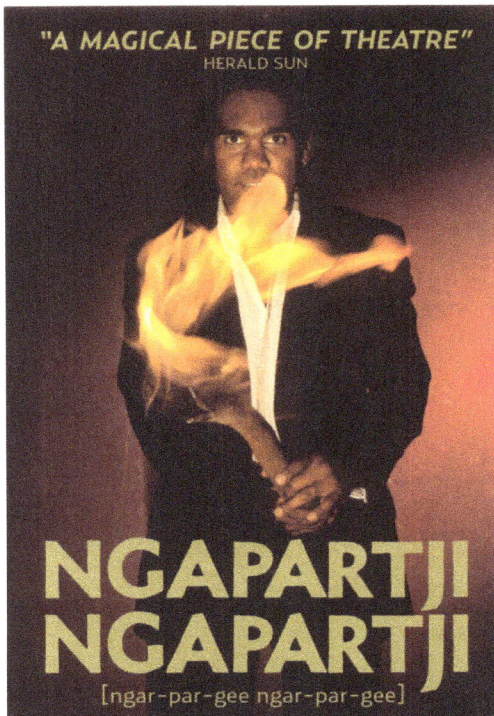

"A MAGICAL PIECE OF THEATRE"
HERALD SUN

NGAPARTJI NGAPARTJI
[ngar-par-gee ngar-par-gee]

NGAPARTJI NGAPARTJI
THEATRE PERFORMANCE POSTER
© NGAPARTJI NGAPARTJI

youth participants. Ngapartji Ngapartji explored alternative approaches to meet the aspirations and literacy needs of Indigenous young adults. The project sought to align learning and arts activity with participants' values, languages, aspirations, and social and cultural practice, while also developing skills and sharing experiences that allowed both participants, and the wider community, to navigate across both cultures (Leonard 2008). The emphasis on multimedia was integral to youth engagement in the project. A variety of media and music workshops and projects were conducted in Alice Springs and in Pitjantjatjara-speaking bush communities. Films were produced for the project website and music CDs were produced for sale.

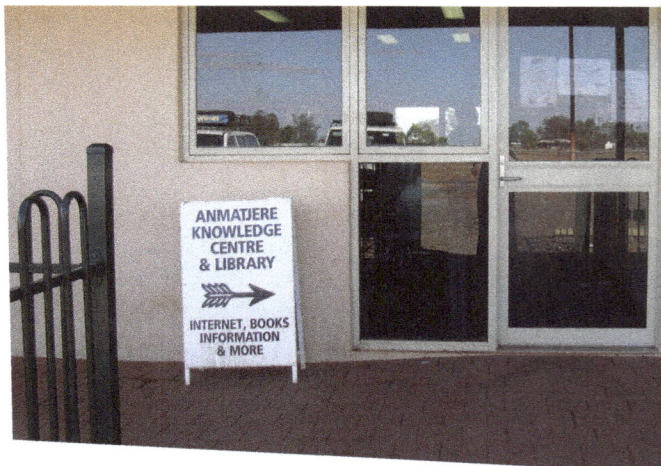

Libraries and Knowledge Centres at Lajamanu and Ti Tree

The Northern Territory Library (NTL) supports twenty two remote community Libraries and Knowledge Centres (LKC) across the Northern Territory. The LKCs combine traditional library services with electronic resources and new media tools. A focal point of this initiative is the *Ara Irititja* digital archiving software, also found in public access locations in the Pitjantjatjara and some Ngaanyatjarra communities (Hughes and Dallwitz 2007), and now rebranded by NTL as the *Our Story* database (Gibson et al. 2011). Working with the LKCs, young people with computer and media skills take responsibility for archiving and documenting community knowledge in databases of heritage materials. In the database repatriated items are enriched with annotations in English or the local vernacular and new material is included through the use of digital media technologies (Gibson 2007).

The involvement of young people in the various LKCs is diverse. At Lajamanu young people (who have developed media skills through 'PAW Media and Communications' based at Yuendumu) worked with NTL to set up the Lajamanu *Nganju Our Story* archival database in the local LKC. Acting with little institutional support, these young people have independently harnessed resources to acquire media skills and produce innovative work linked directly to a broader community commitment to language and culture maintenance.

Throughout 2008 and 2009, a group of Batchelor Institute for Indigenous Tertiary Education (BIITE) students worked on an oral history project with Margaret Carew in the *Own Language Work* course at Ti Tree. Young women documented accounts of life on cattle stations establishing this history as an important part of local Anmatyerr identity. A collaboration with NTL through the Ti Tree LKC ensures that the oral histories are archived in the *Anmatyerr Angkety* (Anmatyerr Stories) *Our Story* database.

I want to learn to read and write for language, culture, so I can teach my kids. It's important so my kids can be strong to speak Anmatyerr when they start working for Anmatyerr culture. English is important too so that they can be teacher.

LANA CAMPBELL
TI TREE COMMUNITY, 2008

I want to do it for my people, especially for Anmatyerr people. Yeah, because they want more young people to work on this. So we can translate it into English, do it in Anmatyerr and translate it into English. It's important.

GAYLE CAMPBELL
TI TREE COMMUNITY, 2008

Youth Programs at Yuendumu, Nyirripi, Willowra and Lajamanu

Youth programs in the four Warlpiri communities (Yuendumu, Nyirripi, Willowra and Lajamanu) are supported by the Warlpiri Youth Development Aboriginal Corporation, Mt Theo – Yuendumu Substance Misuse Aboriginal Corporation, and the Warlpiri Education and Training Trust (WETT).

In addition to sport and recreation and other programs, the youth programs provide regular access to computers so young people can use *iTunes*, download digital photos, and write texts. The Mt Theo program includes the *Jaru Pirrjirdi* (Strong Voices) Project. *Jaru Pirrjirdi* supports the development of young adults aged 17-30 years of age by providing a challenging and progressive framework through which young people can move forward. It achieves this by providing a range of programs and a community service structure through which youth can engage in meaningful and productive community activity.

In July 2008 WETT, in collaboration with the Mt Theo youth program and PAW Media and Communications, implemented a youth and media program for 12 weeks a year for youth in all four Warlpiri communities. The youth program identifies young people who are engaging with the program and those that want to learn more about media production with the idea that they may move onto employment with PAW Media or elsewhere. In this way the youth program is creating training and employment opportunities

for youth in remote communities through a media pathway. The program is expanding to include new types of media training to support youth to re-engage with education, enrol in media and other courses (e.g. Batchelor Institute or Charles Darwin University in the NT), or to get a job in their own community. In November 2009 PAW Media commenced a 'train the trainer' program focused on animation and digital storytelling providing youth workers and local trainees with skills to continue activities and training other young people in the Warlpiri communities (WETT 2010).

**YOUTH CENTRE,
WILLOWRA COMMUNITY**
PHOTO: YOUTH LEARNING PROJECT

Ngaanyatjarra Media at Wingellina

Ngaanyatjarra Media is located at Wingellina in Western Australia, some 700 kilometers from Alice Springs. Since 1992 Ngaanyatjarra Media has been responsible for radio, film, and music production, broadcasting and training, as well as the promotion of language and culture maintenance in the three languages of the region: Pitjantjatjara, Ngaanyatjarra and Pintupi.

Around 2003 Ngaanyatjarra Media established a 'telecentre' in Wingellina followed in 2005–06 by online 'media centres' in other Ngaanyatjarra communities (Featherstone 2011). These sites provide public access computers containing information and applications that are meaningful to local people. Now people have access to computers to view and create their own photos, music and media content. They also use the

internet to search online for cars and musical instruments, download songs from *iTunes*, do internet banking and communicate with an ever-widening network of friends on *Facebook*. In the media centre at Wingellina, computer engagement incorporates the *Ara Irititja* archival database of digitised heritage materials.

In December 2006 informal training workshops in *GarageBand* (free software available within the multimedia *iLife* suite on Apple Mac computers) were held for local young musicians in five Ngaanyatjarra communities. After only a few days training, young musicians had developed sufficient skill to start recording, producing and teaching others. The potential enterprise pathway of this nascent music industry is being explored by Ngaanyatjarra Media through a three-year regional music development program. Locally produced CDs are advertised on the internet and distributed for sale in Aboriginal music retail outlets. The distribution potential in the international world music market remains, as yet, untapped.

> In addition to *GarageBand* and *iPhoto*, the *Ara Irititja* computer is just the best media application I've seen out here...and the best way to engage people with computers without actually identifying it as a computer.
>
> **DANIEL FEATHERSTONE**
> CO-ORDINATOR
> NGAANYATJARRA MEDIA, 2008

Alice Springs Public Library

The Alice Springs Public Library provides an Indigenous-friendly environment where Aboriginal people of all ages can access digital and textual resources. In particular it is a space where young people can access computers, the internet, wireless TV and music systems, videos and DVDs, as well as books, magazines, pencils and paper. The *Akaltye Antheme* section has Indigenous-oriented books, magazines and the 'Indigi-links' computer network. In the databases of historical photos people can find photos of themselves and their relatives. In this way Indigenous language and culture is affirmed in the public space. There are few other public locations in Alice Springs where Aboriginal people can feel as comfortably and confidently located.

While observations were carried out at Alice Springs Public Library, there were no youth participants from this site involved in the research project.

Old way of schooling not working, we need a new way for these kids. These kids are not going to school anyway, but in the library doing activities that are making them proud, giving self-esteem and saying "I can do this". We don't tell 'em it's a learning environment, we just do it...when they have access to resources they write things.

INDIGENOUS LIBRARY WORKER
ALICE SPRINGS, 2008

ALICE SPRINGS PUBLIC LIBRARY
PHOTO: YOUTH LEARNING PROJECT

LEARNING SPACES AND PRODUCTIVE LEARNING

Before expanding on the forms of *productive learning* that became apparent in the research we wish take one step back and situate this discussion within the context of the shifting nature of cultural production in the remote Indigenous context.

NEW FORMS OF CULTURAL PRODUCTION

Indigenous youth are now encountering a greater range of lifestyle options and future choices than ever before. They are exploring and internalising new and diverse 'intercultural arenas of social practice' to forge an emerging identity based on a multiple influences (Merlan 1998: 145). They are negotiating and traversing new pathways towards the meaningful practice of everyday life that differs markedly from that of previous

NEW FORMS OF CULTURAL PRODUCTION
PHOTO: ANGELA HARRISON

First of all you must never forget who you are, *yapa*, Warlpiri man or woman, then have your feet planted in two worlds, whitefella way and our way. Computer skills are very important. But don't forget who you are, always think you are a *yapa* first, follow two roads, if you don't know one from the other, well you won't be a good leader. If you know both worlds you'll be able to be the bridge between two cultures.

GEOFFREY BARNES
WARLPIRI LEADER
LAJAMANU, 2008

generations. Although the socialisation practices and the acquisition of the skills and cultural competencies required for adult life have altered, the values, norms and dispositions transmitted across the generations remain linked to the Aboriginal worldview.

As in many Indigenous cultures around the world the old modes of cultural production, including the chores and tasks that previously filled up everyday life, are no longer perceived as 'work' in contemporary life (Katz 2004). Although many in the older generation in remote communities may still participate in traditional modes of cultural production—hunting, gathering, artefact making and so forth—on a regular basis, this is no longer essential for survival. By contrast, the everyday activities of the youth generation have diverged from cultural norms, and this has led to a tension associated with how time should be spent and the kind of activities that give life meaning and purpose in the everyday and across the lifespan. Where in the past young people were enculturated into skills and practices that made sense in the traditional cultural context, in today's world the Western 'school to work transition' model is pervasive. Yet, often it does not match the social, cultural or economic reality of community life (Fogarty 2010; Kral 2010a; Schwab 2001). Some anthropologists

NATALIE O'TOOLE AND CHRIS REID
FROM WINGELLINA COMMUNITY
PHOTO: YOUTH LEARNING PROJECT

have addressed this issue by claiming that 'many Aboriginal people don't especially like participating in Western institutions', especially the institutions of education and employment (Burbank 2006; see also Austin-Broos 2003 and Tonkinson 2007). While this may be true, we argue that there is value in exploring the nature of productive learning and the multiple pathways to employment and enterprise generation they often entail. In fact as our study indicates, many young people are already leading the way. They have deeply immersed themselves in various forms of productive learning that are meaningful in the remote context and are attractive to young people.

As mentioned above, digital technologies are transforming the nature of communication, leisure, learning and employment world-wide. Indigenous youth are connected to this globalised media world where new technologies are enabling innovations in multimodal communications, cultural production and enterprise development. This is having a profound impact on the kind of productive learning we are describing here. In the learning spaces we describe below, access to resources is enabling the generation of new modes of cultural production that often incorporate and celebrate Aboriginal language and culture. The individuals we portray are determining the areas of specialisation within media production that most interest them, while simultaneously drawing ideas regarding content, quality and expertise from local sources and global youth culture. These new forms of cultural production are legitimate activities that mirror contemporary

circumstances. That is, the skills and competencies they are developing incorporate the technological learning required for altered recreational and employment futures.

Internationally, researchers have noted the shifting role of formal education and the heightened importance of informal apprenticeships in people's everyday lives (Barron 2006; Buckingham 2008a; Coy 1989; Greenfield 2009; Lave 2011; Seely Brown 1999; Summerson Carr 2010). Importantly, these informal apprenticeships typically arise in community-based learning spaces where young learners are 'voluntarily developing expertise' (Heath 2010: 8). With access to learning spaces and control over various media, young people around the world are experiencing what it is to participate in non-directed learning, to practice that learning and through internal monitoring and self-evaluation to produce meaningful cultural artefacts. The kind of learning illustrated in this volume reflects the patterns of informal learning, apprenticeship and voluntary specialisation development that will increasingly prevail in communities and workplaces around the globe.

New spaces for productive learning

As researchers we approached the project sites outlined above as contexts for understanding learning in community-based or informal learning contexts. Gradually we started to view these sites as *learning spaces*, as sites of situated learning and productive activity. The learning spaces we identified in this project appeared in:

- ▶ Community arts projects
- ▶ Libraries
- ▶ Youth Centres
- ▶ Media Centres
- ▶ Digital networks
- ▶ The spaces beyond

While each of the first four of these has an identifiable base or building or physical space in which young people participated in learning, we observed an important non-physical space that was equally and sometimes more important: Digital networks. Digital networks are a virtual rather than geographically anchored space accessible through electronic networks of various new media. These non-physical spaces can be accessed through computers, the internet and mobile phones. They are just as significant as sites of learning and creative production as are the physically bounded sites. Indeed for many young people they are increasingly and sometimes more important. Finally, we also observed productive learning in what we characterize as 'the spaces beyond'—community learning spaces beyond the buildings and the confines of a 'nine to three' school day or a 'nine to five' training and employment routine.

Indigenous youth are moving swiftly and continually through these 'spaces beyond' as they orbit between the learning spaces of home, the bush, the ceremonial ground, the sports ground and so forth integrating these fields into new modes of learning via digital media production and sharing.

The tools and contexts of productive learning

Within each of these learning spaces, and over extended periods of observation, we saw Indigenous young people engaged in 'communities of practice' (Lave and Wenger 1991) where productive learning took place. We documented the many ways in which youth are participating in new arenas of learning and production: language and cultural knowledge recording; film making; music production; theatre performance; and enterprise development and organisational learning. Importantly, what we discovered was that youth in remote regions are learning how to use and manipulate new digital technologies at an astounding rate. This remarkable change in socio-cultural practice is also impacting on the way that young people are using multimodal literacies in new and innovative ways. In the learning spaces we observed, individuals collaborated, experimented, acquired and shared skills, knowledge and expertise, gained confidence, assumed new roles and responsibilities, reconfigured their identities and created new knowledge, art and commercial products. Based on our observations we will now discuss the productive learning that emerged from the various learning spaces.

Many of the learning spaces we observed provided a locus for communal after-school and night-time activity. In particular, media organisations, youth programs, and arts and community development projects have tapped into digital media as a way of engaging young people in meaningful productive activity in the out-of-school hours. Activities are typically unstructured and participants choose what to do and when, and they can leave and return as many times as they like, depending on what else is happening in the community. In such locations young people have been introduced to computers through the multimedia Apple Mac iMovie and iPhoto applications and computer games. Multimodal practices are learned in digital film-making and music workshops. Competence is gained informally through observation, peer learning, trial and error, repetition and interactions with non-Aboriginal mentors. In some locations young people are engaging in video-making using cameras and complex computer editing programs and producing and distributing DVDs of their work. In others they are composing, writing and recording songs using the *GarageBand* software on Apple Mac computers and producing CDs and music videos.

In what follows we describe the practices, process and outcomes of productive learning in the various learning spaces. We do not, however, attempt to define the specific features or characteristics of, for example, the media centre as learning space. The physical setting is not so important as the productive learning the space facilitates. We have both observed media centres in communities that are well stocked with high technology equipment yet no productive learning takes place there. In many important ways the physical setting is necessary but not sufficient to engender productive learning. In the remainder if this chapter we explore some of the productive learning that emerged from the various learning spaces we identified. Specifically we introduce the productive learning being generated as a means for engagement with the outside world, visual storytelling and cultural work and music and media creation.

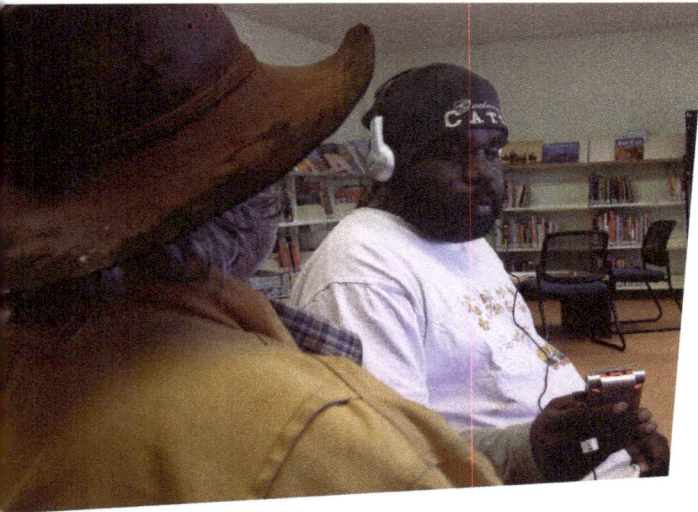

New technologies and engagement with the world

Digital technology is now firmly part of everyday practice: Indigenous youth don't need to be taught it, they are just doing it. Even in communities with no mobile phone coverage young people walk around with mobile phones viewing photos or videos and listening to music. With increased personal ownership of small mobile media technologies and greater access to resources in the sites described above, young people are producing and controlling new and unique art and information. Music and video recordings, packaged with artwork and lyrics for sale and/or uploaded to the internet, have been common to most of the projects. The character and shape of these creative,

> People became less fearful of the technology and through that process of engaging with it learnt more so that sense of knowing how to use and manipulate technology, for your own gains for your own means, it became much more user friendly.
>
> **ANNA CADDEN**
> WETT MEDIA TRAINER, 2009

cultural productions are particular to each locale. In all the sites learning is not based on a programmatic curriculum, but is integrated into and contextualised around real life. Through a process of iterative engagement young people are showing that they are fearless of technology Importantly young people are walking in the door and choosing to participate because these cultural production roles are in the domains of knowledge that matter to them—culture, arts, country, and new technologies, within a framework of social relatedness. Importantly, these small technologies—and their linkages through the internet and social media like *Facebook* and *YouTube*—also enable engagement with the outside world, with young people and other cultures far outside the home community.

In these learning spaces young people are typically introduced to digital technologies through 'mucking around' with *iTunes* and digital photos, often on old personal computers. Initially this learning does not require high levels of technological comptence as learners can employ visual, spatial and motor skills for clicking, dragging, cutting and pasting images, text or sound. Skills are initially acquired through observation and imitation of those more skilled. Then individuals practice. This is an important first step in young people gaining independent, non-directed computer experience and problem-solving confidence. Embedded also is a high degree of regular reading and writing of song titles, playlists and music genres, often through copying, cutting and pasting and determining song repeats and multiple copies. In some locations young musicians were observed repeatedly listening to songs in the *iTunes* playlist to determine how songs are constructed and to mimic the drum beats. In others, young people listened to and transcribed songs from *iTunes* then typed and printed good copies.

Later, and in collaboration with mentor experts in short-term workshops or project-based learning activities, young people acquired a higher level of technological competence in video production, computer editing and music recording using software such as *iMovie* and *GarageBand*. Early productions included digital storytelling and non-narrative iMovie compilations with multimodal layering of image, text, song and gesture. Eventually, individual specialisations started to emerge and innovations occurred as young people experimented with digital technologies. In their determination to perfect their newly acquired expertise young people spent hours in recording studios, arts centres and old radio broadcasting rooms.[4]

Some participants have had little or no schooling, and a history of petrol sniffing or getting into trouble. Through youth media projects they develop personal strengths and new technical skills and literacies. As young people's skills expand some are called on to participate in community projects as camera operators and editors or to compile CDs of their songs for distribution beyond the local community. Meanwhile others have expanded their networks through presentations at conferences and symposia in urban centres. Importantly, in many cases young people have continued on to formal training in media work or language interpreting courses at BIITE and have found work in their areas of specialisation. Others are participating in enterprise generating projects or have moved into full-time employment and community leadership positions.

It's really important that people have access and there's amazing ways of learning, problem solving, creative thinking. One of the most special outcomes of media work is that people can adapt that thinking and problem-solving to everyday stuff outside. I see those guys grab a video camera, they co-ordinate it, they're talking to each other, they're directing it as well as filming it and editing it. There's a lot of strong communication skills coming out of that. Strong leadership skills. Technological side, using computers. Computer is just a tool to get that idea in your head, that movie happening. A new tool, a new form, a way to share your vision.

MICAH WENITONG
YOUTH WORKER
YUENDUMU, 2009

Editing, making movies, whole process of filming and recording and cultural learning going on. Then you've got the technological learning going on with the camera. And the computer skills and everything after with the editing. And that's very popular, using technology to engage learning of culture... Young people feel control and ownership because they are the ones that know about the technology and the new media. And the old people have their role as they know about cultural knowledge.

AMY HARDIE
YOUTH WORKER
WILLOWRA YOUTH CENTRE, 2009

I found computers easy for me, like to type and do everything on the computer, everything like doing internet banking and helping other people in how to use the computer in the Telecentre. I do some works for the Telecentre and for the Media, sometimes when I'm bored I come to the Telecentre, sit down, play around looking there, do good things, then learn more good things. I like checking my emails, Yahoo, and I like to do some photo decoration on the computer, on the Publisher, scanning photos.

NATALIE O'TOOLE
WINGELLINA COMMUNITY, 2008

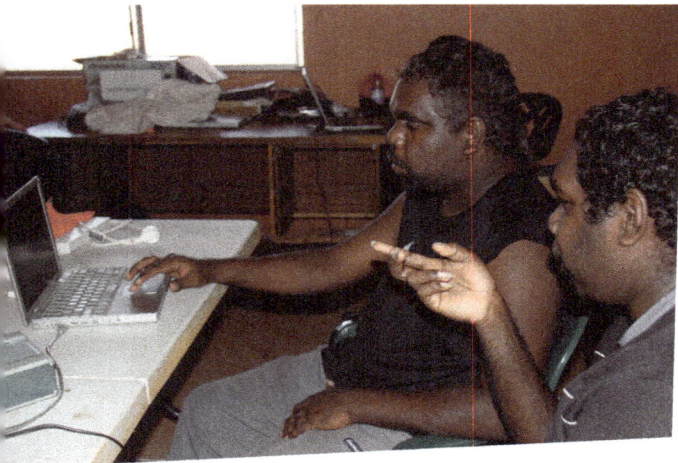

Visual storytelling and cultural work

In Lajamanu, youth media workers Shane White, Maxwell Tasman and others have acquired media skills through non-formal training with Warlpiri Media (now known as PAW Media and Communications), as well as observational learning and participating in a range of community media projects. Shane and Maxwell have made films with old people on country, and worked on documentaries for Aboriginal organisations, media organisations and the LKC.[5] In the LKC Shane and Maxwell have learned how to import media items, understand file formats and add metadata and they work with elders to record, transcribe and translate texts:

> We've got to learn from the old people, but we have to learn how to put it into the database for Warlpiri people and everybody really.

Recently they have been employed through the Central Land Council to film two DVDs documenting the WETT-funded community development activities.

Participating in these projects has given Shane and Maxwell a respected role as filmmakers. Simultaneously, they are acquiring cultural

knowledge by working directly with elders. These young men are independently accessing film-making resources in the 'old BRACS room' in Lajamanu in order to edit music videos and cultural documentaries, often adding subtitles in Warlpiri or English. These contemporary digital artefacts are placed in the *Our Story* community database in the LKC. In their spare time they make films for fun so that they can learn more by 'mucking around' with camera techniques and editing using *Final Cut Pro* film editing software. As Shane says,

> I do media work because I enjoy it and I love editing. We have open access to the BRACS room, we use the equipment anytime we want. I like making people laugh, do a bit of dance videos, music videos for the Library Knowledge Centres or put them on *YouTube*.

Shane and Maxwell have now commenced formal media training through BIITE and are employed by the Central Desert Shire.

At Djilpin Arts, young film-makers Amos Urban, Ricardo Weston and Revonna Urban have worked for a number of years with Julia Morris, a visiting non-Indigenous mentor film-maker. They have gained media skills through participating in community media projects. In these projects they are given responsible roles where they interact and communicate with Indigenous and non-Indigenous mentors and film and edit professional standard films.

You can learn both ways, you can learn *kartiya* way, learn technologies, computer all that stuff with media, reading all the numbers, lights, reading books...And learning *yapa* side, even the birds, and plants, yeah even the season, looking at both ways.

It bring two ways together...And that's the best way to learn...We got all these things, like technology, we can record all these story, video, songline everything...when we go, as long as we leave something behind so all the kids can look after it and so they can pass it on...to the next generation...we knowing this technology like media, started knowing this, started use this thing in the right way because old people going away. From knowing this media I'm starting to know these old people and knowing what they got... and knowing all that stuff what you learn from both ways ... the time will come round that you start teaching and you start taking the responsibility.

MAXWELL TASMAN
YOUTH MEDIA WORKER
LAJAMANU, 2008

When you look at technology, which in a sense is all about communication in one form or another, I think what has been sorely missing is that communication between mainstream Australia and remote communities...Shane and Maxwell are perfect examples of tackling that head on in the sense that they are really clued in and think: "How can we tell stories which other people will understand?", you know "How can we bridge this gap between the cultures that exist in Australia?". They see technology and media as a way of doing that...They are after this connection and the connection is communication, bridging that gap and making life better for people in communities.

ANNA CADDEN
WETT MEDIA TRAINER, 2009

They [Shane and Maxwell] are learning really well from me and my father and all the old fellas. Maxwell's someone who you thought "Oh he's not gonna learn anything!". But no, now he got this passion of learning and doing things the right way, he's become a good example for people...He's an example, like I said, he was someone who got no hope, yeah, hardly doesn't take his own culture or anything seriously, *yuwayi*. But after he learned why all the *yapa* culture is all about connections. Oh he wants to prove himself that he can make a difference. And you know, he's been doing it, he always going to teach young fellas too...Shane was a quiet one, but he was really good at computers. But he's another one, didn't take his culture seriously. But you know, in his own way, his body language and everything saying now "I've gotta start becoming more"...So Shane more quiet, but he wanna prove that he can make a difference as well because he believes in that sort of teaching... I want them to be anything you know, I want them to take advantage of all the opportunity, all that thing. I even like to see them go overseas and make a difference over there. But, one thing, they must come back and still tell me that they can sing that song for that bird or sing that song for that tree, *yuwayi*, that tell me that they still know who they are.

STEVE JAMPIJINPA PATRICK
WARLPIRI EDUCATOR AND LEADER
LAJAMANU, 2008

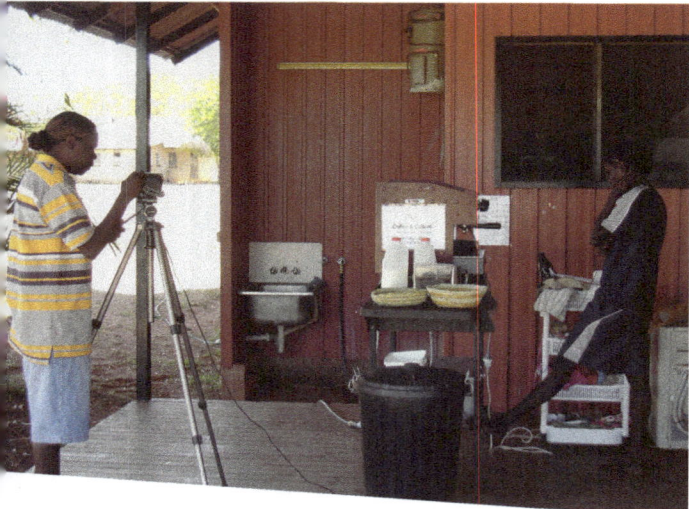

DIGITAL CULTURE, WUGULARR
©DJILPIN ARTS

Projects are multiplying and young people are taking on new roles as film-makers, writers and directors and producing music videos for sale. Amos and Ricardo are now employed by Djilpjn Arts to document the arts and cultural activities in the community, including producing broadcast quality music video clips. Amos has also been employed by other organisations to film cultural activities outside of the community. Recently, Revonna's film *The Boss for his Country* was aired on ABC TV's *Yarning Up* series of Indigenous films.[6]

At Ngapartji Ngapartji, in addition to participating as performers in the theatre performance, young people like Belinda Abbott, Joanne Andrews, Julie Miller, Sadie Richards and Maureen Watson engaged in creative multimodal activities through non-formal media training workshops with Ben Foley from the Central Australian Aboriginal Media Association

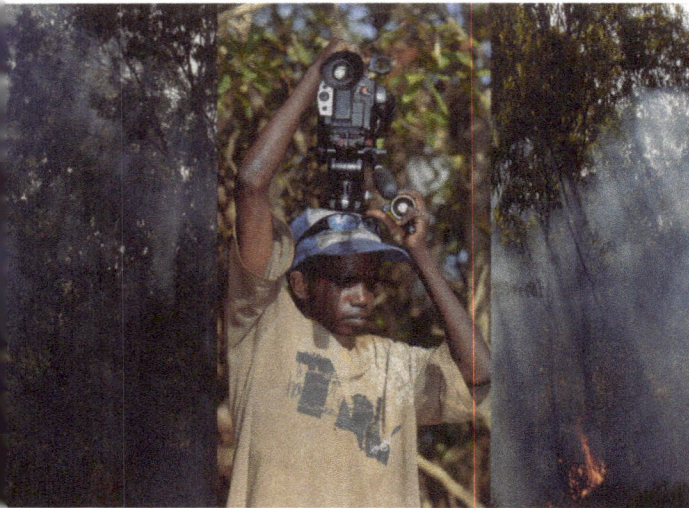

REVONNA URBAN FILMING AUGUSTINA KENNEDY,
WUGULARR COMMUNITY
PHOTO: YOUTH LEARNING PROJECT

Different work we have: media and festival. And I'm learning how to be a Manager, running the Arts Centre and making sure all the art workers, we all work together you know. I think it's really important that we keep our culture strong. And my other job is working with Julia, doing the media with some of the younger people like me. We have four music video clips. I made one documentary about my grandfather. It's called *Boss for his Country* which is for this place and I showed it at the Festival—*Walking with Spirits*—and I was so excited to see it!

REVONNA URBAN
BESWICK COMMUNITY, 2009

They're making their own music, they're making film clips... these girls, oh they are just amazing. As soon as they got given that tool of talking in front of a camera they came out more. So the more experience they get behind the camera or in front of a camera organising their own little lives around that, you know if we just give them like a guideline to use, say "Here look, this is the idea, see if you can pull out something from your own selves, but this is the idea, we'll give you the camera and make yourself a film."

TREVOR JAMIESON
CO-CREATOR
NGAPARTJI NGAPARTJI
THEATRE PERFORMANCE, 2008

Someone like Maureen was interesting because we met her out on country where she lives when we were doing filming stuff and she just stood out as being really interested. She had lots of ideas, she was a leader. So we sort of promoted her in that role, storyboarded with her, got her to say what she thought the other young people should do. She was really outstanding and she ended up editing with Suzy and doing subtitles and saying how she wanted her film to be.

DANI POWELL
ASSISTANT DIRECTOR
NGAPARTJI NGAPARTJI
THEATRE PERFORMANCE, 2008

Media and arts skills, strongest way of people learning and young people can share their stories and communicate...capacity to learn is enormous with media...people want to do it, they want to share their story and see what it looks like. Important for people to want to do something, opportunity for people to fulfil their own dreams and do stuff they enjoy.

MICAH WENITONG
YOUTH WORKER
YUENDUMU, 2009

(CAAMA) and by 'mucking around' by themselves on the computers at Ngapartji Ngapartji in Alice Springs or in video workshops with Suzy Bates in Pitjantjatjara-speaking bush communities like Ernabella and Docker River. Activities included making films for the Pitjantjatjara language learning website, producing slide shows and digital stories and recording music and producing CDs. The nature of these processes enabled participants with low literacy to express themselves in their own languages, with images and voice rather than the written word. The recent award winning feature film *Nothing Rhymes with Ngapartji* portrays the project and attests to the important role played by young people in this significant cultural production.

Music production and new technologies

Access to new digital technologies has led to an explosion of musical creativity and productivity across remote Indigenous Australia. Ngapartji Ngapartji rode the wave of this interest and music was an integral component of the critically acclaimed *Ngapartji Ngapartji* theatre performance. In addition, the arrival of powerful yet accessible computer-based recording technology underpinned song writing and music and film recording workshops in Pitjantjatjara speaking communities that led to the production of a number of CD compilations: *Ngurakutu Ara Desert Reggae* and *Wanti Watjilpa*. At Djilpin Arts, collaborations between traditional songmen and Western musicians provided a focus for the annual *Walking with Spirits Festival* and the production of innovative CDs and award winning traditional and contemporary dance and music videos.[7] As noted above, at Lajamanu filmmakers

teaching and ongoing practice; this is possible because the technologies are accessible and the production challenges meaningful and relevant.

At Wingellina, musicians Nathan Brown and Chris Reid thrive on learning, but their learning process is hidden away in a makeshift 'recording studio'— an empty room with an iMac computer, a mixer, a pair of speakers, an electric guitar or two and some old furniture. The nonchalant manner of these young musicians belies the fact that when writing, producing and recording their music they work intently toward perfection. Through hours of practice they hone their skill. In the studio they rework tracks over many hours and days of improvisation, experimentation and recording and rerecording until a song is considered finished. These young men are fearless of the

Shane and Maxwell have been filming and editing dance and music videos with local musicians and producing DVDs; many of which have been uploaded to *YouTube* and then shared with the local community via mobile phones using bluetooth technology. Collaborations with local musicians 'The Lajamanu Teenage Band' and Callum Scobie are enabling others to observe and join in the productive learning associated with multimedia cultural productions.

The adoption and use of *GarageBand* software in the Ngaanyatjarra Lands is emblematic of the ways in which Indigenous youth are rapidly gaining expertise in using and manipulating new technologies in community-based learning environments. After an initial introduction to the *GarageBand* music recording technology by John Gordon, an expert non-Indigenous trainer, young musicians quickly assumed control over the recording and subsequent production. These learners, many of whom have incomplete schooling and varying levels of literacy competence in English and Ngaanyatjarra, are setting high skill attainment levels for themselves that are not based on a programmatic system of institutional learning. Rather, they are learning by observation, trial and error experimentation, peer

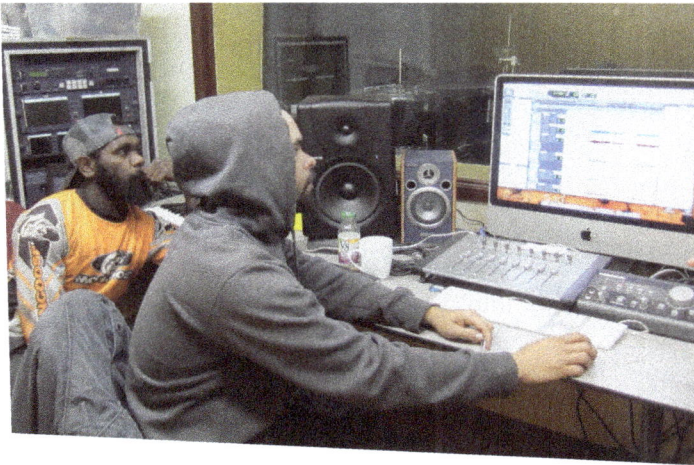

technology and this fearlessness is allowing them to stretch the boundaries of what is possible and to find myriad innovative ways of achieving the oral/aural outcome they imagined before entering the recording studio. As Chris describes:

> We can make different sounds now, like we learnt more. Now we can make our own sound. Like keyboard sound, we used to copy sound from other bands but we can make our own tune, our own style of music now. They heard the bass, that sound that we were doing and now other bands copy our style. They use our sound now.

Their band, the Alunytjuru Band, plays live in local festivals, but with *GarageBand* software they are now able to independently record and produce, distribute and sell their music and reach a much wider audience.

The use of music recording software like *GarageBand* requires not only a facility with computers, but also some level of alphabetic and digital literacy, problem-solving, decision-making, and acute listening skills. With *GarageBand* the visual interface on the screen uses a familiar symbol system and recognisable icons (mirroring those found on cassette players or video cassette recorders), enabling even those with limited English literacy skills to quickly get the hang of it. There is no such thing as a mistake as everything can be deleted and reworked. "It doesn't matter", Chris remarks, "we learn from making mistakes". The symbolic conventions used in applications such as the spatially-oriented and icon-based

structure of *GarageBand* are enabling users (who previously may have avoided text-only procedures) to interpret, read and manipulate technology. In doing so, young people are elaborating the spatial and symbolic dimensions of familiar communication modes and adapting them to new media activities. Recently, the construction of a new professional standard music recording studio at Ngaanyatjarra Media in Wingellina has enabled young musicians to move to the next level where they are now using *ProTools*, the industry standard audio recording software used by engineers and producers around the world.

In summary, the learning spaces we observed commonly incorporated the arts—music, theatre or multimedia—alongside digital technologies. The productive activities within those spaces often drew on Aboriginal language and culture and linked closely with local community interests and needs. It is clear that a vibrant learning environment often multiplies opportunities for engagement across and beyond the local community and sometimes nurtures the development of new enterprises. What we have

It's like this is something that whitefellas have developed as some sort of level of fear or respect for computers, that it's somehow sacred territory, it's not out here, it's kind of fair game, whatever you can get into and change around you do so...if there's information that's relevant and meaningful to people in the box, then they will find a way to get to it, in the same way that people will learn to fix a car if they know that that car is going to get them to where they want to go. So it becomes not so much how to learn the technology but actually creating something that's meaningful to people.

DANIEL FEATHERSTONE
CO-ORDINATOR
NGAANYATJARRA MEDIA, 2008

Not only from the school they are learning, but from outside the school. Like in the Telecentre, like in Irrunytju young boys, well only young girls are going to school, like around about 13,14,15, young people at that age, especially, only the girls are going to school, but young boys aren't going to school 'cause maybe they think it's boring at the school. So yeah, so they are interested in other things like music, doing music on the computer, *GarageBand*, or learning other good things from the Telecentre or from the Media.

NATALIE O'TOOLE
WINGELLINA COMMUNITY, 2008

learned and what young people have shown us is that learning is most effectively fostered through interest-driven engagement in projects and activities that matter to young people, and that these learning spaces effectively stimulate the acquisition and development of language and multimodal literacies, organisational learning and social enterprise.

In the next chapter we further explore the underpinnings of learning spaces and link these specific and localised examples of productive learning to both a series of important national policy questions and to a growing international body of theory on the nature of learning, literacy, youth and media. As we will show later, by placing the examples of productive learning we have observed among Indigenous young people in an international and theoretical context, it is possible to identify key features and underlying processes of productive learning that can be incorporated into everyday practice as well as the design of learning spaces.

CHAPTER 2 ENDNOTES

1. See discussions about youth ambivalence and resistance to schooling in mainstream contexts (Bottrell and Armstrong 2007; Corbett 2004; McKendrick et al. 2007; Smyth and Hattam 2004).

2. Geoff Lohmeyer, youth worker, interview 2008.

3. In addition to government funding Djilpin Arts has been supported by The Fred Hollows Foundation, Ian Thorpe's Fountain for Youth and Caritas Australia.

4. In 1987 the former Broadcasting in Remote Aboriginal Communities Scheme (BRACS) was implemented, representing a federal government response to the perceived threat to Indigenous languages and culture posed by the new the national Australian AUSSAT satellite system. Through BRACS, equipment and training were provided for the production and broadcast of local community radio and video services for insertion over the incoming mainstream services now being beamed from AUSSAT (Deger 2006; Rennie and Featherstone 2008).

5. Film projects include: the DKCRC/PAW Media *Stories in Land* film; documentation of the Milpirri Festival with the community and Tracks Dance Company from Darwin; and assisting visiting researchers with recording elders singing traditional song cycles.

6. *Yarning Up* creates screen industry development and employment outcomes in remote Indigenous communities. *The Boss for his Country* was directed by Revonna Urban and produced by the Top End Aboriginal Bush Broadcast Association (TEABBA) in association with NTFO, Screen Australia, ABC Television, NT Department of Education and Training (DET) and National Indigenous Television (NITV).

7. Muyngarnbi Music Videos from Walking with Spirits won 'Best Traditional Recording', NT Music Awards 2008; and 'Best Music Video' ImagineNative, Toronto 2008.

CHAPTER 3

LEARNING SPACES: FROM THE LOCAL TO THE GLOBAL

DIGITAL CULTURE,
NYIRRIPI COMMUNITY
PHOTO: JANE HODSON

In this chapter we seek to connect the applied aspects of learning spaces and productive learning described in the last chapter with an internationally emerging body of research and theory related to literacy, learning, media, youth and identity. To demonstrate the links between what we have observed in Australia and what is being explored overseas, we have organised the chapter around a series of what we believe are significant questions.

If remote Indigenous communities are to overcome their economic disadvantage and political marginalisation they will require skilled individuals who can facilitate a strategic articulation with mainstream Australian society. Similarly, if young people in remote communities are to become competent, mature adults able to shape their own futures and the economic and social viability of their communities it is essential that they have access to learning experiences that will contribute to the formation of a positive sense of self, strong cultural identities, and independent learning and literacy skills.

In most public commentary and policy debate, schooling—and the attainment of English literacy—is promoted as the singular pathway to successful futures in remote Indigenous communities. Almost invariably, that success is defined in terms of employment and participation in the 'real economy' (Pearson 2000). Consequently, enormous political and financial investments are being channelled into early childhood, school, and vocational education and training (VET) programs in remote areas, but to now most results have failed to meet expectations. Research on literacy in the Indigenous context tends to focus on schools with a particular emphasis on teaching methodology, curriculum and outcomes. What little is known about adult literacy in remote Indigenous communities indicates that literacy levels are low and the lack of literacy is affecting the ability of Indigenous people to participate fully in employment, to the degree employment is available in those communities (Kral and Falk 2004; Kral and Schwab 2003) Cross-sectional, synchronic assessments of English language and literacy in instructional settings are not only problematic in terms of what they are actually assessing among school children, but they also provide no insight into the maturation of skills across the lifespan. In fact, few studies ask what happens to language and literacy once acquired (Heath 1997). We argue that it is important to know what happens to young people after they leave institutional learning environments and what they take with them into their futures and across the life course:

▸ how they use literacy in everyday life;

▸ how they acquire new learning as systems and technologies alter;

- what experiences lead to leadership roles, further education and employment; and

- what factors lead to successful life outcomes and adult well-being.

As researchers we have looked to theory in anthropology, sociolinguistics and human development to help us answer these questions and to make sense of what is going on in the social context that we are examining. To do this we have focused our attention on what *is* happening, not what is not. What we have found is that what is happening—and our insights and conclusions—is often in conversation with international theoretical developments.

WHAT'S THE DIFFERENCE BETWEEN LEARNING AND SCHOOLING?

Policies and programs too often equate 'learning' with 'schooling' but these are fundamentally different things. School is a limited institution, both temporally and socially, but learning is a fundamental feature of human life. As John Singleton once wrote,

> ...schools are complex social institutions, not general models of education and learning. If anything, they are extreme— and unlikely—models of enculturation. From the early acquisition of language to the later induction into occupation and social roles, we learn by observing and enacting social roles in everyday social contexts. Learning is situated in communities of practice, and schools are very limited as such communities. We

do learn to be students in school, but we learn to be adults in adult society. (Singleton 1999: 457)

As mentioned earlier, a basic tenet of anthropology is that cultural forms are transmitted from one generation to the next through enculturation or socialisation as well as direct and indirect teaching and learning. Socialisation can be broadly defined as 'the process through which a child or other novice acquires the knowledge, orientations, and practices that enable him or her to participate effectively and appropriately in the social life of a particular community' (Garrett and Baquedano-Lopez 2002: 339). Direct teaching using a Western model of 'schooling' or institutional learning was introduced into remote Indigenous society relatively recently—in some communities only within the last 50 years or less. Consequently, there has been a profound shift in socialisation and learning processes among remote groups within only a few generations. Learning previously relied solely on observation, imitation and guided participation through everyday social practice in the company of elders within a hunter-gatherer existence; colonisation introduced a sedentary Western-oriented lifestyle pivoting around learning from outside experts within institutional frameworks. The taken for granted role of schooling in remote contexts is rarely questioned. However, in our minds understanding the links between culture, learning and language and the sites in which learning is situated requires a view of learning that extends beyond the traditional frame of 'the school'.

WHAT ROLE DOES LANGUAGE PLAY IN LEARNING?

Most importantly, the process of socialisation is realised to a great extent through the use of language, as language is 'the primary symbolic medium through which cultural knowledge is communicated and instantiated, negotiated and contested, reproduced and transformed' (Garrett and Baquedano-Lopez 2002: 339). This process, referred to as 'language socialisation', is the lifelong process whereby social and cultural practices and understandings shape the way that people acquire and use language within the local culture or speech community or 'community of practice' (Schieffelin and Ochs 1986).

Researchers in language socialisation have drawn on theory from anthropology and sociolinguistics to examine how learners acquire the knowledge, practices and dispositions required to function as competent members of social groups and cultural communities. Language socialisation researchers have addressed the fact that for many people and communities today language socialisation involves not only the co-existence of more than one language or dialect. It is also commonly mediated by new information and communication technologies (ICTs), and may involve the development of related oral, written and multimodal, as well as cultural, practices intertwined with new intercultural or 'hybrid' identities (Duff 2008).

Until relatively recently, for many Aboriginal people in the remote regions of Australia, the production and reproduction of linguistic forms was linked to a nomadic lifestyle where language skills, strategies and attitudes were tied to a predictable framework of practice. Now in the remote Indigenous context, socialisation processes have often been deeply affected by changing access to stable family lives and the changing structural features of local communities. Social relations and the practices of cultural production and reproduction have altered. Aboriginal adolescents are now more distanced from traditional language immersion contexts than ever before. Indigenous Australian languages are in a state of language shift, with some endangered (Australian Institute of Aboriginal and Torres Strait Islander Studies with the Federation of Aboriginal and Torres Strait Islander Languages 2005) . Former language socialisation processes are fragmenting and traditional oral practices are diminishing (Simpson and Wigglesworth 2008); adult vernacular communicative competence is seen as less relevant for contemporary conditions and circumstances. Simultaneously, with the predominance of English in the domains of education, employment and the media, many young people have internalised the message that only English, rather than their mother tongue, has value. Yet many Indigenous children and adolescents are failing to acquire good communicative competence in Standard Australian English (SAE), leaving them 'without a coherent encircling structure of language socialisation' (Heath 2008: xii).

This highlights a significant question underpinning our research: how will Indigenous youth develop the communicative competence and discourse practices required to undertake the important transition from adolescence to adulthood in the globalised digital world?

HOW IS LANGUAGE RELATED TO THE ACQUISITION OF ADULT ROLES?

International research indicates that learning and language socialisation continue well into the adolescent years (Heath 2008; Hoyle and Adger 1998) and adulthood as verbal and written registers and styles are acquired according to emerging roles, identities and practices (Heath and McLaughlin 1993). In fact, only during older childhood and adolescence do speakers begin to encounter to a substantial degree the styles, registers, and genres of discourse that advance negotiation, exchange, knowledge acquisition, and skill build-up. These syntactic and discourse structures, as well as their supporting symbol structuring, provide young speakers with the linguistic and conceptual tools to move toward adult roles as workers, parents and community leaders. School is an important site for the acquisition of these structures; however even in mainstream monolingual contexts schooling alone cannot provide the highly complex and intertextual structures of discourse required for later language and literacy development for adult

communication needs.[1] This dilemma is amplified in remote Indigenous communities where teaching is in English as a second language, and school attendance and retention rates are low. Accordingly, significant language development opportunities for older children and adolescents must come from their time beyond classrooms.

International research indicates the importance of collaborative projects with adults for adolescent language development where young people are given responsibility for adult roles and in the performance of such roles practice a broad range of lexical and syntactic structures, registers and genres (Heath 1998; Heath and Smyth 1999; Tannock 1998). Heath has noted the importance of youth engagement in collaborative tasks with adults in youth-based organisations. It is in cross-age tasks that require planning, practice and production work that young people 'receive authentic practice of linguistic structures that reflect planning ahead, linking current actions to future outcomes and self-assessing and self-correcting their own behaviors and attitudes' (Heath 1998: 217). Moreover, Heath continues, if adolescents have few opportunities to engage in joint work tasks with adults, their language use and development will be affected.

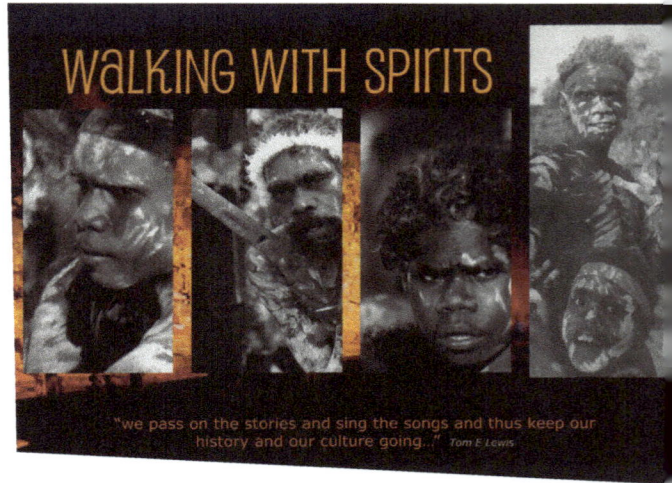

WALKING WITH SPIRITS

"we pass on the stories and sing the songs and thus keep our history and our culture going..." *Tom E Lewis*

WHERE AND HOW DOES LEARNING ACTUALLY TAKE PLACE?

Linguists and anthropologists have opened up new understandings of the interrelationship between culture, language and literacy with the application of ethnographic methods to the study of communication (Gumperz and Hymes 1972; Heath 1983). A range of theories have also shaped understandings of learning and literacy. Vygotsky's 'activity theory' is for many teachers and researchers the foundation of current thinking about learning and human development with its emphasis on socially mediated learning (Vygotsky 1978; Wertsch 1985). More recently many theorists have drawn on anthropology and sociolinguistics in forging a situated and social perspective on participatory learning that broadens notions of learning beyond formal instruction and advances the notion that learning and literacy are purposeful, context-specific and socially organised practices. As a result, a divide has grown between those who see school as the primary site for learning and others who have developed a social theory of learning (Lave and Wenger 1991; Rogoff et al. 2003) encompassing a view of learning through social practice. Such writers emphasise that literacy is not only an instructional process, but also a cultural process and that 'everyday practice' is a more powerful source of socialisation than intentional pedagogy (Lave 1988: 14). In other words, in addition to instruction in school, it is ongoing out-of-school social practice across the lifespan that determines competence:

Humans need to practice what they are learning a good deal before they master it. Furthermore, they tend to lose a good deal of their learning—including school learning—when they cease to practice the skills associated with this learning in their daily lives. This is why it is easy to discover many adults who are no longer very good at school-based science, math, or literacy if they do not, in their work or home lives, practice these on a regular basis. (Gee 2003: 68)

Our work starts with the observation that learning is enhanced where the links between content and context are acknowledged and supported. From this point of view, learning is situated and experience is the foundation of learning. Our research has been deeply informed by the notion of situated learning and its emphasis on engagement in learning at all stages of life. When learning is viewed as 'situated activity' and the focus is shifted from individual skills acquisition to focus on competence and expertise, one can clearly observe that learning is derived from 'participation in the social world' (Lave and Wenger 1991: 43).

Lave and Wenger (1991) have provided specific examples of the situated nature of learning in their descriptions of the process of apprenticeship in various cross-cultural contexts. What emerged from those studies was insight into the process whereby in each setting knowledge and competence was actively gained and expressed initially—through observation and later through participation—in some valued enterprise or activity. Their work involved a significant extension of the notion of situated learning as not merely learning situated in practice, but as 'an integral part of generative social practice in the lived-in world' (Lave and Wenger 1991: 35). Their major insight was the development of an analytical viewpoint on learning, employing the concept of 'legitimate peripheral participation', essentially a rich and insightful description of the process of various forms of apprenticeship through which individuals become members of communities of practice. The process of legitimate peripheral participation involves learners who are recognised as having a legitimate right or responsibility to initially observe and over time engage in activities, construct and employ artefacts and acquire knowledge and skills. In this process learners are on a practical social learning trajectory among a community of practitioners— first as observers, then as competent members, and ultimately as creators and transformers of knowledge and relationships in communities, society and culture. Other scholars have affirmed the benefits of learning through observation and participation in collaborative activities (Paradise and Rogoff 2009; Rogoff et al. 2003).

This focus on the socially situated nature of learning draws attention to the learner as a member of a socio-cultural community, a member of a 'community of practice' (Engeström 1987; Lave and Wenger 1991; Wenger 1998). This theoretical perspective draws learning out of the conventional confines of formal teaching, prescribed curricula and attainment of individual outcomes and qualifications and embraces a notion of meaningful learning that is connected with, and of value and relevance to, the social community to which learners belong. Importantly, it denies the binary of 'informal' versus 'formal' learning and with it the assumption that if a person is 'educated' or 'learned' they have gone to school. Rather it asserts that learning is not in the transfer of abstract or even traditional knowledge but in the socially situated production of knowledge. Accordingly, and in our research, we have found it is far more instructive to engage in an exploration of the 'doing' of learning... than focusing on (didactic) teaching as the cause and condition of possibility for learning' (Lave 2011: 144–145). In our experience, 'learning' is 'context-embedded'; it is found in the situated *doing* of life. In this way, and most importantly, it is inseparable from the learning space and the practically situated processes of production, observable in our project in the various creations of film, music, dance, theatre and enterprise by the Indigenous young people who shared with us their practice.

OK. BUT LEARNING 'WHAT'?

Theoretical models of learning have become more sophisticated over time, reflecting deeper understandings of the nature of learning, but also the ways in which learning has itself changed shape as the social and technological world has become more complex. Douglas Thomas and John Seely Brown suggest that learning has had a different focus over time (Thomas and Seely Brown 2009). At the beginning of the twentieth century, learning was broadly conceived of as a process for the formal acquisition of knowledge. What needed to be learned was stable, as were the contexts within which that learning took place; learning was essentially 'learning about'. This fitted the needs of rising industrial nations and framed the delivery of education in public schools. A major shift in understanding of learning came through the work of Lave and Wenger and others which, as noted above, demonstrated the situated nature of learning and its social construction. Critical to this reconceptualisation of learning was recognition of the process whereby individuals gain some practical and socially valued competence through observation and action. According to this view of learning, individuals are enculturated into skills and practices that enable not only participation but also 'learning to learn'. This notion of learning included the various forms of apprenticeship that take place outside 'school' and which result in not just the acquisition of knowledge and skills but of a new role in practice.

Thomas and Brown refer to this as 'learning to be'. Both of these conceptions of learning assume a relatively stable environment, with a sense of permanence and continuity over time. A new focus on learning, they argue, is required to accommodate the increasing instability and change of the twenty-first century. 'Learning to become' is what is required in a world where knowledge and skills are not static, where the content of what one has learned and the learning trajectories through which one learns that content are continually replaced and realigned as once constant contexts now continually shift. Learning today and into the future is a socially situated process and practice of becoming over and over again. This is no less true for Indigenous youth as they struggle to become the leaders of tomorrow and the guardians of cultural knowledge.

FIGURE 1.
THE EVOLUTION OF LEARNING
[THOMAS AND BROWN 2009]

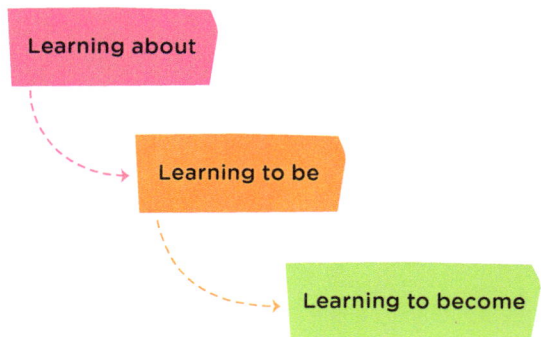

Learning about

Learning to be

Learning to become

HOW IS LEARNING LINKED TO IDENTITY?

The phrase 'learning to become' expresses well the inextricable link between learning and identity. On one level a person's identity is defined in relation to others, but also identity is formed and performed in a fundamentally social process of 'self-making' in interaction with others (Bartlett 2007: 53). Identity is constantly shaped, negotiated and enacted. It is contingent and elastic, in a constant process of formation and change (Mallan et al. 2010: 268). We have observed among the young people participating in this project what Lave and Wenger (1991) have described as the clear link between learning and identity. We have watched individuals work together in various learning spaces. We have observed the acquisition of new technological skills and new literacies. We have watched as they gain confidence, solve problems, create knowledge and assume new responsibilities. As Bartlett and Holland show, to learn is to become a different person (Bartlett and Holland 2002). In other words, learning and the acquisition of various literacies is not just about acquiring new skills but also about changing identity and representations of self (Barton et al. 2007: 210). In this sense learning has a trajectory. While our research is not a study of Indigenous identity, the ways in which young people engage in learning and with multimodal literacies appears to be a process whereby they shape and reshape their senses of self, often in positive and socially affirming ways.

Internationally, conventional understandings of identity are being challenged as new media provide a new fluid and flexible space for expressions of self where 'individual' and 'technologies' converge (Mallan et al. 2010: 264). In our research we have observed Indigenous young people enter the global space of *Facebook* and *YouTube* posting films and music they have created with digital technologies, identifying themselves as fathers, mothers, musicians, entrepreneurs, cultural custodians and much more. They are building social networks and portraying their lives, their cultures and their countries to each other, to other Indigenous people and to the world, in a way that would have been unforseeable a generation ago. What is most impressive is the skill and confidence they present in these media. They portray not only their individual personalities and creativities, or their Aboriginal identities and cultures. They also display what Lave and Wenger have termed 'identities of mastery' (1991: 85), as we note with musicians learning the *GarageBand* software. They are skilled and clever participants in both the local and global world, enacting an expertise that is recognised both in their remote home communities and increasingly in the outside world.

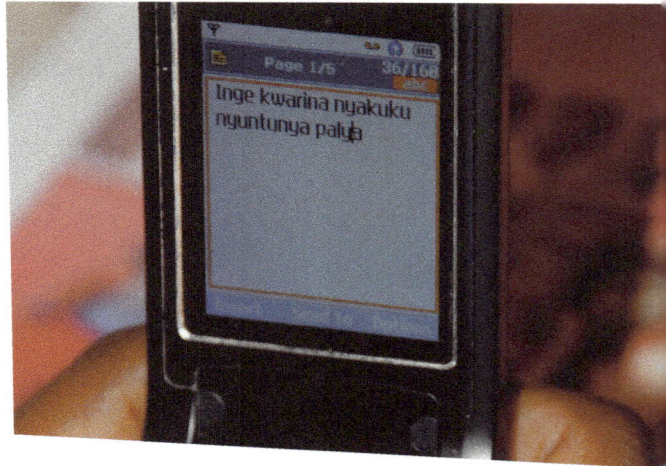

HOW IS LEARNING LINKED TO THE DIGITAL WORLD?

Among the most significant features in the contemporary world are digital networks and new media. By definition these technologies dismantle boundaries of time and space and have propelled change across the globe. From the perspective of our project, young people in the geographically remote communities with which we are working are active participants in this world and they have become, in less than a generation, participants in projects, productions and communications that would have been not only impossible but literally unimaginable twenty years ago. The implications of these changes for conceptions of learning are profound and illustrate the relevancy of Thomas and Brown's notion of 'learning to become'.

Digital media and networks are increasingly prominent features of this constantly changing world. These developments are extremely significant for understanding the nature of learning today in that they have enabled new and pervasive forms of what Wenger, McDermott and Snyder refer to as 'knowledge-based social structures' (Wenger et al. 2002: 5). These digitally-based structures challenge existing notions of communities of practice in that they often involve extension of communication outside the local community (e.g., via film or music recordings) and/or the creation of multiple and varied virtual spaces where young people can interact (e.g., *Facebook*). As a result, as James Gee (2005) suggests, understanding

(and supporting) learning requires a focus on the 'space' where people interact rather than their membership in a local community situated in a physical or geographical location; he refers to such spaces as 'affinity spaces'. This idea fits well our experience and understanding of new media and the nature of learning among young people in remote Aboriginal communities, and we include them as a particular type of learning space.

Gee's analysis of learning within affinity spaces also aligns with our own observations of learning among young Indigenous people engaged with digital media. In these places and in these spaces, learning is fundamentally different from what takes place in schools. While school learning is increasingly focused on 'learning about' (as assessed by NAPLAN tests and the like) learning spaces are sites where young people are 'engaging with information and use it *in a broader social context* as a crucial part of... productive inquiry' (Thomas and Brown 2009: 3, emphasis in original). That productive inquiry is part of the process of 'learning to become', of assuming responsibility and shaping images and stories and interacting with the outside world.

The engagement of young people with digital media illustrates the nature of the process of 'learning to become'.

> Young people today are confronted with and enter more and more affinity spaces. They see a different and arguably powerful vision of learning, affiliation and identity when they do so. Learning becomes both a personal and unique trajectory through a complex space of opportunities (i.e., a person's own unique movement through various affinity spaces over time) and a social journey as one shares aspects of that trajectory with others (who may be very different from oneself and inhabit otherwise quite different spaces) for a shorter or longer time before moving on. What these young people see in school may pale in comparison (Gee 2005: 231)

EARLY DESIGN FOR THE 'YOUTH LEARNING' POSTER
PHOTO: YOUTH LEARNING PROJECT

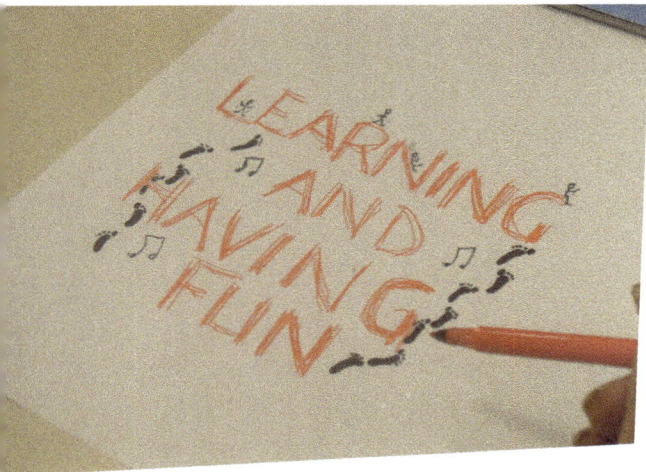

HOW ARE THESE NEW MEDIA LINKED TO LITERACY?

The rapid development of ICTs, an increase in affordable, small mobile technologies and the penetration of the internet and mobile telephony over the last decade account for an explosion in new modes and channels for communication and multimedia production. Digital technology is altering styles of engagement and learning and catalysing computer mediated communication and multimedia cultural production outside institutional or instructional settings. Internationally, such developments have led to substantial ethnographic inquiry (Buckingham 2008b; Hull 2003; Ito et al. 2010) into youth and the emergence of changing social practice surrounding new media and have led to new understandings of language and literacy. Socio-cultural learning theory (Lave and Wenger 1991; Rogoff 1990) looks to everyday social practice in out-of-school settings for models of learning and engagement (Hull and Schultz 2002) that differ from what is typically found in instructional locations such as schools or training. This approach aligns with a growing literature examining the relationship between online communication and changes to alphabetic reading and writing conventions (Crystal 2008) and language use in new media settings (Jones and Schieffelin 2009; Thurlow and Mroczek 2011). International studies (Hull 2003; Soep 2006) suggest that fresh thinking about literacy has been ushered in by the arrival of digital technologies and the emergence of changing social practice surrounding digital technologies.

Writers comment that mobile phone messaging and online writing is strengthening and enhancing our language abilities (Baron 2008). Others note that youth uptake of informal forms of writing in online contexts is part of a broader set of social and cultural shifts in the status of printed and written communication (Ito et al. 2010). An affordance of computer mediated communication is its multimodal aspect (Kress 2010) evidenced in the increasing prevalence of 'multimodal literacies' that draw on a variety of communicative options including speech, writing, image, gesture and sound (Hull and Nelson 2005). Computer mediated communication requires a reframing of what is meant by literacy in a globalised world increasingly 'filled with digital artefacts and multiple modes and media available for communication across multiple symbolic systems' (Stornaiuolo et al. 2009: 384).

In remote Indigenous Australia a digital divide is evident in many locations (Daly 2005; Rennie et al. 2010), nevertheless altered individual and collective youth media practices have developed in accordance with broadband, satellite or Wi-Fi availability (Featherstone 2011). Communication using mobile phones, texting and online communication via social networking sites is becoming central to everyday practice for Indigenous youth. As we note, public access sites such as libraries, media organisations, youth centres and arts programs are providing important collective lifespan learning spaces in locations where there is minimal engagement in formal education and training. The developing ICT competence of young people is defining a generational identity distinct from that of their elders, with digital media representing an arena where youth can exhibit technological expertise that exceeds that of the older generation.

In the digital environment, learning a new procedure, performing technologically complex tasks and participating in new modes of cultural production can be mediated in ways that do not necessarily privilege alphabetic written systems. While multimodal practice benefits from the intuitive meta-textual skills of alphabetic literacy, such practice also incorporates gesture, signing, gaze, eye contact and haptic or kinaesthetic aspects. The creative, icon-based approach embedded in the Mac *iLife* suite of applications lends itself to a rich layering of image, sound *and* text. Hence, young people who have familiarity, though not fluency, with standardised alphabetic symbols find it relatively easy to work out how to navigate their way through the icons and symbols to construct texts and engage with creative cultural production (e.g., producing music and editing films).

Digital media technologies have engendered an explosion in multimodal literacies among youth who have access to the new tools of production—computers and mobile phones—enabling the generation, dissemination and decoding of multimodal texts. The visual-spatial and symbolic conventions used in online and new software applications are enabling users to interpret, read and manipulate technology in personally and socially meaningful ways. Despite the assumed dominance of English in digital media and online

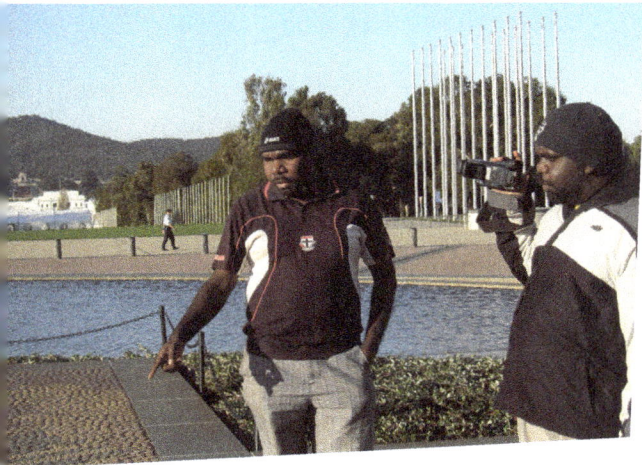

practices, the content of many multimedia activities is enabling some young people to extend their vernacular literacy skills in song-writing or transcribing and translating subtitles for films.

To sum up, Indigenous youth in remote communities are encountering a complex of competing and conflicting language socialisation influences and learning and identity formation pathways. These young people are finding they must balance traditional socio-cultural obligations with the increasing requirement to participate in the wider Australian community. New understandings of what it means to participate in activities and relationships across social, geographic and historical time and space, and into imagined futures, must be developed and enacted through language and other meaning-making systems. We suggest that innovative ways of thinking are needed to address how Indigenous youth will develop the communicative competence and discourse practices they will require to undertake the important transition from adolescence to adulthood in the globalised digital world. Building on the theoretical models outlined in this chapter, we now move onto a range of practical suggestions or design principles for thinking about youth learning in out-of-school settings.

Chapter 3 endnotes

1. Shirley Brice Heath, pers. comm., August 2008.

CHAPTER 4

DESIGN PRINCIPLES FOR INDIGENOUS LEARNING SPACES

In this chapter we apply what we have learned from international theory and research to what we observed in the various learning spaces and what Indigenous young people shared with us.

Though we want to emphasise again that we don't believe a single replicable model is possible—or desirable—we have identified what we believe are a series of design principles that can be of value in building or facilitating learning spaces:

- ▶ Design Principle 1:
  A space young people control

- ▶ Design Principle 2:
  A space for hanging out and 'mucking around'

- ▶ Design Principle 3:
  A space where learners learn

- ▶ Design Principle 4:
  A space to grow into new roles and responsibilities

- ▶ Design Principle 5:
  A space to practice oral and written language

- ▶ Design Principle 6:
  A space to express self and cultural identity through multimodal forms

- ▶ Design Principle 7:
  A space to develop and engage in enterprise

- ▶ Design Principle 8:
  A space to engage with the world

ARNHEM LAND BILLABONG PHOTO: YOUTH LEARNING PROJECT

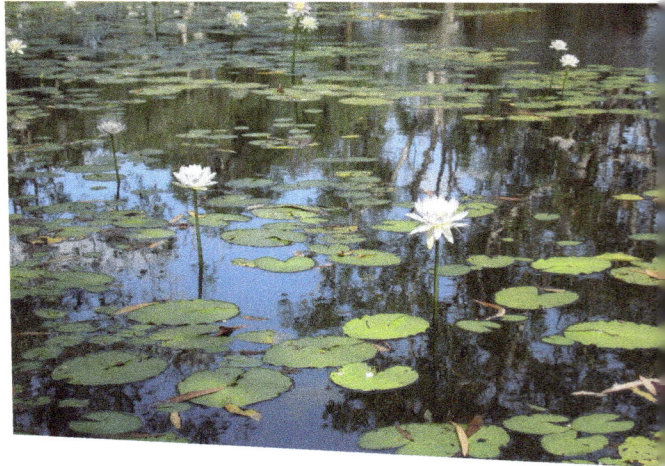

DESIGN PRINCIPLE 1:
A SPACE YOUNG PEOPLE CONTROL

In most remote Indigenous communities 'learning' is typically controlled by institutions: the school, a training provider or a workplace. Some great individual teachers notwithstanding, these institutions almost invariably assume a deficit perspective, where Aboriginal people are seen to be lacking not only in skill but also interest and commitment, never meeting national benchmarks or achieving mainstream standards of employment participation. Within these institutions new non-Indigenous teachers and trainers come and go with numbing regularity, arriving and departing with low expectations of Indigenous educational capacity and engagement. The outcome of all this is predictable. In most communities and small townships with a large Indigenous population, adolescents are early school-leavers or are not attending regularly, and many struggle to make the transition from school to work.

Most Aboriginal people who live in remote communities (and in towns) are painfully familiar with racism and discrimination, and the sense of disempowerment and marginalisation that accompany them. Even those who remain in their home communities have firsthand experience of the incremental erosion of personal control over many aspects of everyday life. New policies and systems associated with welfare benefits, education and local government are often framed as returning responsibility to Indigenous people and communities, but many are punitive (for example, linking welfare payments to school attendance) and ineffective.

There are few spaces in the public domain where Aboriginal people experience a sense of control. If they venture into towns a subtle yet pervasive racism precludes them from comfortably accessing public facilities like banks, cafes, and even the public swimming pool. In many communities—and even towns—there are few public access spaces where Aboriginal people can engage in informal personal, recreational, functional or informational reading and writing activities. This is mirrored in the domestic domain. In many homes books, pens, paper, children's educational resources or computers—all the resources taken for granted in the literate middle class domestic environment—are not readily available.

It is well known that access to resources engenders the kind of home literacy practices that are the antecedents to successful literacy learning at school (Teale and Sulzby 1986; Wells 1985).

In middle class literate homes children (and adolescents) are socialised into particular types of language and literacy practices (Duff and Hornberger 2008). They observe their elders reading, writing and undertaking the administration of everyday life, as well as engaging in talk around text. Children from such homes are therefore more likely to absorb literacy as a taken-for-granted practice and continue to use reading and writing in the post-school years:

> Children who learn to read successfully do so because, for them, learning to read is a cultural and not primarily an instructed process. Furthermore, this cultural process has long roots at home—roots which have grown strong and firm before the child has walked into school. Children who must learn reading primarily as an instructed process in school are at an acute disadvantage. (Gee 2004: 13)

Access to resources and a space that is conducive to the enactment of literacy practices is therefore a critical yet virtually unrecognised factor in the education debate in remote Indigenous Australia. In the remote context where Aboriginal people feel marginalised in the public domain and have minimal access to literacy resources at home, community-based organisations like youth programs, libraries, arts projects and media centres play a critical role in providing a space where resources for alphabetic *and* digital literacy development and independent learning can be accessed.

So the short films we make with them we put on DVD and give back to every participant so they can watch them at home on a DVD player. Computer access seems really hard, like communities I've been to we tend to go in school holidays and we say "Have you got a computer?" and they say "There's some at school but they're locked up in the schoolroom." Obviously you've got to keep them safe, except Docker River there's one computer sort of in a cage in the rec hall so supervised people can go and use that. In terms of what other young people in the country have got with the computers at school and stuff it's really limited.

DANI POWELL
ASSISTANT DIRECTOR
NGAPARTJI NGAPARTJI, 2008

People do appreciate that things at the Youth Centre get looked after. Like people have had laptops, but they've lasted like a week and they bring it down to you and it's broken. But people know that they can always use a computer at the Youth Centre and that it's looked after and that it's for everyone…And people will often leave stuff at the Youth Centre on the basis of knowing that it will stay safe there.

AMY HARDIE
YOUTH WORKER
WILLOWRA YOUTH CENTRE, 2009

Importantly, these are sites where Aboriginal people, especially young people, feel a sense of spatial control. It is in these locations that young adults not only have access to resources that enable, as we discuss below, 'learning by mucking around', but also input from mentor experts to expand the development of specialised expertise.

Community-based organisations provide a location where people feel supported and systems and procedures become more transparent. Dani Powell from Ngapartji Ngapartji suggests that the core of community-based organisations like Big hART is that youth participants experience 'agency':

> …to feel that you don't always have to be like that [marginalised] and you know how to move into that other world with confidence. And it doesn't mean you become an actor like Trevor [Jamieson], but it means if someone says "We can't go in there, that shop or whatever", you go "Yes we can, we'll go in, I know how it works".

The strong message that the youth performers who toured to capital cities with the *Ngapartji Ngapartji* show imbibed was that they were respected by non-Aboriginal people in a manner rarely experienced in Alice Springs. As Director Scott Rankin noted: "When they come to Sydney people want to talk to them, they are like stars."

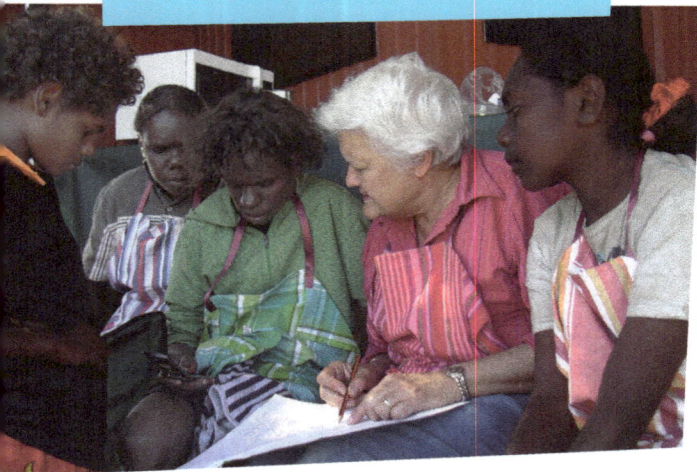

YOUNG PEOPLE LEARNING NEW SKILLS AT GHUNMARN CULTURE CENTRE, WUGULARR, 2008
PHOTO: YOUTH LEARNING PROJECT

I try and expose young people to everything I'm doing. So if I have forms, like money forms that people have to sign I make it really simple so they can read it and sign it. Or I show them how other people did that, or I'm writing out the timetable. I make a big schedule and I always look at it myself and I noticed that one young woman was getting curious "What's that?" she'd ask. And I went "Why don't I make you one, here it is and let's go through it". She was desperate to know: "What are we doing tomorrow?" ...It's that stuff you need to know to feel more access and control, not people have got the knowledge and they're not going to tell me. It's a sort of moving outside passivity, being moved around, but if I know what's going on I can start to plan and manage my own time here.

DANI POWELL
ASSISTANT DIRECTOR
NGAPARTJI NGAPARTJI, 2008

NGAPARTJI NGAPARTJI **THEATRE PERFORMANCE, BELINDA O'TOOLE AND ELTON WIRRI WITH ELDERS**
© KEITH SAUNDERS

SCENARIO
NGAPARTJI NGAPARTJI THEATRE PERFORMANCE, SYDNEY, JANUARY 2008

On stage Trevor Jamieson introduces Elton Wirri as Albert Namatjira's grandson. At this moment the audience's attention is drawn to a young Aboriginal man who has been quietly drawing a landscape in white chalk on a black wall on the edge of the performance space. Immediately by referencing this iconic Aboriginal artist, young Elton is transformed from a somewhat invisible Aboriginal youth into a symbol of unfulfilled artistic possibilities, now a young man of status and potential.

NGAPARTJI NGAPARTJI **THEATRE PERFORMANCE, BELINDA O'TOOLE AND SADIE RICHARDS**
© KEITH SAUNDERS

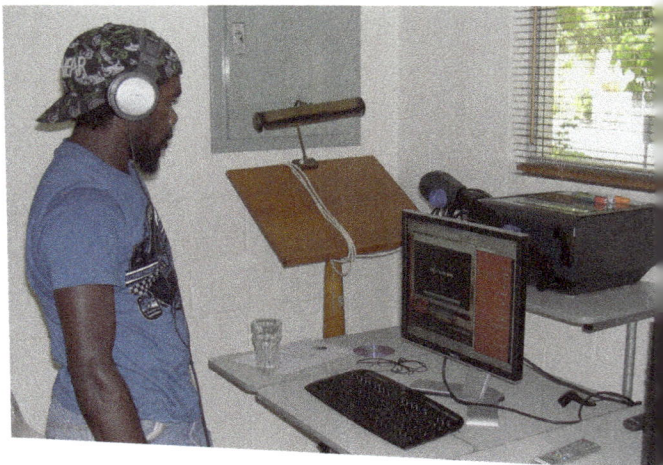

Although access to technology in many remote communities may still be mediated through a non-Indigenous 'gatekeeper', the emergence of affordable small, mobile digital technologies including mobile phones, digital cameras, mp3 players and even laptop computers has brought technology into the everyday lives of Aboriginal people, especially young people. This has shifted the control of technology away from organisations and non-Aboriginal authorities and placed it in the hands of Aboriginal people. Now young people are doing things—by themselves— that previously would have been unimaginable. As a consequence young people's capacity for technological learning and practice is expanding. Even those with low levels of literacy are quickly able to grasp the intuitive problem-solving logic of small media devices and computers. As Youth Media Trainer Anna Cadden suggests, Aboriginal people today 'have a lot more confidence around technology generally':

> People will have personal individual mobile technology because they can keep it safe or they can keep it in their pocket and it's theirs. Mobile technology has brought technology into people's homes...So I think that's influenced that accessibility and therefore that understanding of the language of technology...that makes it easier as well for people to understand technology outside of those mobile devices.

As one facilitator suggested, even the experience of control over the smallest choices (down to the level of fonts, titles or colours) in a computer-based activity may increase a sense of confidence that extends to enacting decisions related to difficult situations in everyday life.[1] Access to resources is therefore an important enabling factor allowing young people to access information and be controllers and producers of knowledge and unique community-valued resources. In this process there is freedom for individual specialisations to emerge and individuals are setting and attaining high level skill and other goals for themselves. The young people in the projects described here are gaining a sense of control over small personal horizons.

Lastly, public libraries play an important role in providing one kind of access point in the public domain where Indigenous people can access learning resources. Public libraries and LKCs are well-positioned to respond to learning and literacy needs, including the new online trend, for *all* ages and *all* groups.[2] The Alice Springs Public Library offers a unique learning space that is well-utilised by Indigenous people, including Indigenous youth, some of whom attend school and some who don't go to school at all. The library atmosphere is atypical, it is cool and quiet, a place for people to access resources in a free, but rule-bound, environment. Library rules are uniform and apply equally to all. The library encourages neatness, books must be returned, paper picked up, and chairs pushed in. It is also a location where Indigenous people can communicate with people of all cultures. Community and town camp people join the library to use the internet and those who know more show others. Young people come in to use computers especially in the *Akaltye Antheme* Indigenous resource section. Even those with minimal literacy can sidestep alphabetic text, and still have meaningful library engagement.

SCENARIO
ALICE SPRINGS PUBLIC LIBRARY

It is a hot quiet Monday morning and some thirty Aboriginal people are in the library. Some people stay in the library all day. A group of older people are quietly watching a video with headphones on, around ten school-age boys are playing computer games in the youth section, four older men are sitting by themselves reading books. It is cool inside and there few places in town where Aboriginal mums and babies can come and just sit. Two young women in their early twenties come in. One young mother has two babies and a toddler. She is also babysitting for her sister who is doing business in town. She finds two story-books and starts reading with the children. After a while she takes the toddlers to the children's section and plays blocks with them. She says she likes coming to the library to read science magazines to learn more. At her town camp there are few learning facilities or resources, especially for children. Around midday she leaves and has lunch on the lawn nearby and later returns to the library for the afternoon.

After lunch sixty or so Aboriginal people are in the library, reading newspapers, books and magazines. Ten school-age kids are playing games on computers in a far corner while a few mothers with babies and toddlers in the children's section. An 18 year old young man from a town camp is using the internet. He says Drop-in Centres are for school kids and there are few places for young adults like him in town. He uses his sister's library card to book time on the internet. He searches for music sites and has worked out how to type in the names by himself. He also follows the links on *YouTube* to watch film clips. As he leaves the internet an American tourist sits down in his place. The tourist asks for help find his Yahoo site. The young man is proud that he has been the expert and that he has helped an older English-speaking visitor!

Last year at the LKC we had some recordings repatriated from the Finke River Mission. They were recordings of old men talking about land rights essentially, relationships to country, that sort of thing. And the old men who were recorded were the grandfathers of a lot of the young people who were working in the library and coming into the library in Ti Tree. So when I brought them up people were very keen to hear them and sat around the computer in the library and listened to them. On my next visit I was told that one of those families had come into the library, they'd moved the audio file from out of the database copied it and put it into *iTunes* with the rest of their music and they were making playlists with some music and some oral histories. So these sound recordings were made in 1975 or something like that so over 30 years ago.

And why I thought this was such a great story was that where this particular family lived was at the creek and there's no power there. So obviously they couldn't play a CD unless they played it in their car or had CD player with batteries. But people were listening to the recordings on the mp3 player, sitting around with headphones, sharing the headphones around, listening to this old man speak. And this was the first time they'd heard him speak for a very long time. Some people had never heard him before, so it was a really poignant moment for everyone. And they wanted to share to with me: "We took that sound file and we put it on the mp3 player and we did this, it was great." So people were really positive about it and I thought it was really innovative.

Yeah, people living in the creek-bed using an mp3 player to listen to an oral history from 1975, it's great! And the old people obviously they were overjoyed, that the young people were interested in listening to this stuff as well. They probably wouldn't have been able to hear it, some of those really old people who live by the creek don't come to the library very much, so it was the young people's only way of sharing that information with the oldies.

JASON GIBSON
NTL MEDIA TRAINER, 2008

In one community the Media Centre is housed in a demountable with one big room with eight PCs and a Mac holding the *Aṟa Irititja* database. Another room is an office and a further big room is a videoconferencing room. All through the morning people wander in and sit and use computers. It is a public access space and a community resource. There is no whitefella gatekeeper determining access, the door is open from morning to evening, including lunchtime. Anyone can come in, an elder says he has just been in to check that young people are using the space properly. The main restriction is no school-age kids between 9am and 3pm. A school-age girl is there and is told to go to school. She leaves for a while, then returns, not having gone to school.

In another community a young woman in her late twenties manages the Media Centre and is responsible for opening the door every morning. She is confident with computers and does the job with a minimum of fuss and little non-Indigenous intervention. She begins the day searching, selecting, copying playlists and moving desktop folders on her own computer. Her adolescent son is not at school and spends the day in the Media Centre with her. People wander in and out throughout the day: playing Solitaire on the old PCs or listening to songs on *iTunes* and downloading music from the *iTunes* library. Two young women spend the morning choosing songs from *iTunes*. They have bought blank CDs at the store and burn the CDs in the Media Centre, label them and take them to play at home. A man in his 50s comes in. He tells the manager what songs he wants and she copies around 40 songs onto his mp3 player. While he's hanging around he takes a photo with his own digital camera. He has with him a small canvas bag with various leads and chargers for his mp3 player and digital camera. At home he has a laptop for downloading photos, playing music, writing reports for his job. Around 4pm the manager organises to go on air with the local radio station 5NPY broadcast across the NPY Lands. She sets up her playlist on *iTunes* a mix of local Aboriginal bands plus some Gospel music and rock and roll. As she plays the songs she makes community announcements in English and Ngaanyatjarra.

DESIGN PRINCIPLE 2:
A SPACE FOR HANGING OUT AND 'MUCKING AROUND'

International research on youth media practice commonly identifies the 'digital bedroom' as one of the most vibrant kinds of digital learning spaces for youth (Jones 2010; Livingstone 2002; Sefton-Green 2006). Here adolescents in advanced industrialised economies can be found 'hanging out, messing around and geeking out' (Ito et al. 2010) with computers, alone or online in small friendship networks, in the privacy of their bedrooms. Adolescents in remote communities generally do not have the luxury of bedroom culture, or access to computers and the internet at home, or garages for teenage bands. Therefore, informal learning spaces such as media centres, youth centres and libraries perform an important function as *communal* 'digital bedrooms' (Kral 2010b). Here activities are public, yet the privacy that is so difficult to attain at home, can be found for individual production and the safe storage of virtual and material texts (in computer folders or memory sticks and locked storerooms). In these spaces electricity and the resources that enable productive learning including computers, cameras, books and even the internet are available, and in working order, for people to use.

Until recently, control of technology was predominantly in the hands of media organisations or community groups. Thus Aboriginal people were typically disengaged from the production process and needed higher levels of assistance. In the BRACS era film-making was more sophisticated, editing was often done by outsiders and then the video cassette sat on a shelf, a detached object, reliant on having a video player and a TV in working order to view it. But with digital media it's all self-contained in the one box where everything can be done: film can be stored and edited, music added, and the edited film can be shown in bite size pieces all in the same computer box. The digital moment has created a process that is much more accessible especially for Indigenous youth. Now a video clip can be made in one day: an idea can be generated in the morning, filmed, edited and completed by the end of the day, then burned onto a DVD and taken home to show family.

Access to what have been termed the 'new generation media centres' in remote communities is recognised as opening up an important collective learning environment for young people to engage, develop skills, create media and increasingly take on professional and leadership roles in their communities (Indigenous Remote Communications Association 2010: 59):

Community media centres are providing a Lifespan learning space in remote communities where there is little engagement in formal education and training. It is a space where remote Indigenous people are interacting on an equal basis with media professionals, without any power differential. It engages all generations in technologically competent tasks of creative cultural production intended for use by the community. (Indigenous Remote Communications Association 2010: 67)

In these spaces 'there is no right or wrong way' for learning or participation and everybody is 'set up to succeed' (Indigenous Remote Communications Association 2010: 67–68).

These are also the spaces that nurture what youth media worker Shane White from Lajamanu terms 'learning by mucking around'. Young people's access to new technologies and control of digital practices is allowing them to gain control, not only over the production process and editing, but also self-representation. Young film-makers are confidently using editing software like iMovie and *Final Cut Pro* to manipulate the medium and the images. As observed by Anna Cadden (interview 2009): 'to have that realisation, not only do you go out with a camera but then you can manipulate these images and you can create a story out of them. And that story can then be shared and it's a way of communicating.'

Learning capacity: to think for yourself, decide for yourself, you have the power to change that whole scene with the edit. You gain the confidence to make those decisions, to stand strong in what you believe and what you see and what you think is best for yourself and other people.

MICAH WENITONG
YOUTH WORKER, YUENDUMU, 2009

Similarly, music recording in the pre-digital era was a long process often controlled by non-Aboriginal 'experts'. Now, young musicians can be the producers as well as the musicians, undertaking the whole process: writing songs down, laying down tracks, and creating text and artwork for CD sleeves all within a short period of time. The *GarageBand* music recording process suits the remote Indigenous context predominantly because the software is relatively indestructible and lends itself to fearless experimentation. Music production for young musicians now requires musicality and creativity *and* computer competence. In the process of music production we are seeing independent and collaborative learning. The *GarageBand* process is providing an opportunity for young men in particular, to privately focus on something that really matters, to do it well, to create their own style and, moreover, to 'shine'. In this private recording environment young musicians seek perfection and rework tracks over many days of improvisation, focused practice, recording and rerecording to create their own unique sound. In this way they experience what it is like to set their minds to something, to practice and to perfect something that matters. Having access to the space, time and resources enabled Wingellina musician Nathan Brown to 'muck around' and perfect his specialisation. According to fellow musician Chris Reid, Nathan 'is good at the computer because he's good at anything':

> With *GarageBand* Nathan already knew he was clever, but other people didn't know he could learn so quick. He likes to fiddle around with things, touching everything, working it out.

Through situated learning, they figured out what to do by 'mucking around'. By using the logic of the symbol system embedded in the *GarageBand* structure, in concert with action and embodied practice (Goodwin 2000), they became as Lave and Wenger state 'learners who understand what they are learning' because they are 'active agents in the appropriation of knowledge' (Lave 1990: 325).[3]

In summary, many young people are structuring their own learning in environments that encourage individual agency and creativity. In these spaces they are free to 'hang out' and experiment and to share and learn from one another. Through everyday exposure to digital technologies they are participating in meaningful everyday learning and practice. These are sites in the public domain where young people can experience a sense of ownership, belonging and control as well as the 'freedoms of time, space, activity and authority' (Heath and Street 2008: 5).

Shane and Maxwell have had the privilege of having a BRACS space there that they really feel ownership over and they look after it. So it is used for work, and for fun and joy and things like that, but it's used mainly for video editing and radio broadcasting. And it's their space, they've taken full ownership over the equipment that PAW placed in Lajamanu and left there for them to use so they've had access to equipment and the computers and they've had a space that they've felt is their own and felt really comfortable in and would go to every day. So in a sense it's that spatial thing and that ownership over the space and that space works in Lajamanu in that sense. The equipment is looked after so there's no worry about what's going on, these guys have a real sense of responsibility over that equipment and it's theirs to play with and work with.

ANNA CADDEN
WETT MEDIA TRAINER, 2009

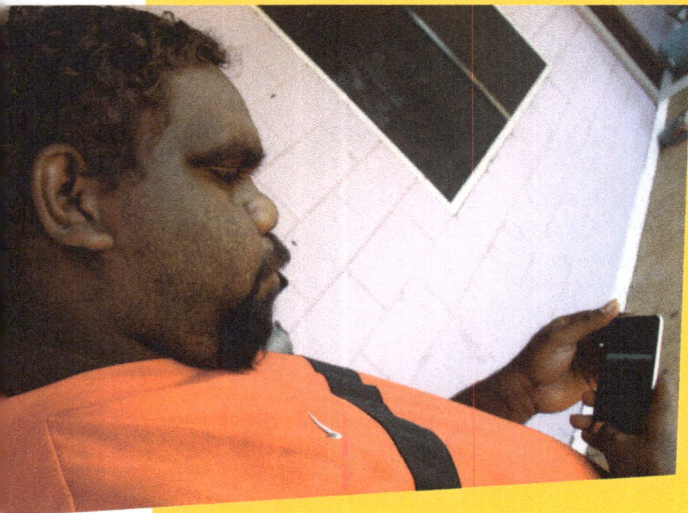

MEDIA HAS CHANGED IN MY COMMUNITY

When I was a child growing up in Lajamanu I used to go and hang out with my friends and make toys out of old tins and wires and play around during the weekend, but on week days I had to be in school because my mother was a Warlpiri teacher.

When I was growing up in Lajamanu I remember we only had a TV and a Cassette player. Then I used to own a walkman. Now I have an iPod, a computer (Both PC and Mac) and a flat screen TV and I also have internet at home and do *Facebook* from my mobile phone.

So Media has changed in my Community.

I remember watching this new channel ICTV (Indigenous Community Television). The first time I saw ICTV I was glued to the TV. It was something new. I liked most of the videos and it made me want to make some videos for my community. Without ICTV I would've been working somewhere different. So ICTV was important for us.

There are now people walking around with iPods and most people have Pay TV and mobile phones. 2 weeks ago when my mother sent me a text message in English, I laughed.

For young Aboriginal media workers like us it's fun and we also learn new things as we are making videos. At the BRACS room where we work, we have keys to go in anytime to use the video camera, people trust us so we have control in the work we do.

SHANE WHITE
YOUTH MEDIA WORKER

(Presentation for the Information Technologies and Indigenous Communities Symposium, Australian Institute of Aboriginal and Torres Strait Islander Studies, Canberra, 2010)

DESIGN PRINCIPLE 3:
A SPACE WHERE LEARNERS LEARN

Thus far we have emphasised how access to resources enables autonomy and agency in learning. We have highlighted the spatial factors that contribute to individual or collaborative voluntary expertise development, or 'learning by mucking around'. In this section we focus on the crucial enabling role played by facilitators or 'expert mentors' in the learning process. While many *un*remarkable adult educators or trainers who impart content from a standard curriculum have come and gone in remote communities, the ones who have the 'magic' stand out. In this research project we encountered many great learning facilitators who planted the seed and nurtured the growth of learning. Although much of what makes a good facilitator is dependent on character and cannot be emulated, a few basic principles apply.

In all of these contexts successful outcomes have been attained through collaborations between Indigenous and non-Indigenous people in the learning process, rather than top-down formulaic training delivery. Such facilitators are skilled professionals. They are passionate about what they do and they love working with Indigenous youth. They have the ability to teach complex technical skills while engaging young adults in projects that entail precision and commitment to completing the task. These facilitators do not see themselves as 'bosses' but give agency to the young people they are working with. They

As a video trainer you are coming in pretty much always to a community for a short period of time to do training and you know it can be quite intense. But what you always have to realise is that you are coming into a community, people live here the whole time, and they have lives outside of the training, so you have to work around people's lives. You can't come in expecting that everyone should drop everything because you are here, you know. "Like they should all come and be trained by me, isn't this a great opportunity and why aren't they doing that?" And those sort of questions don't make a lot of sense when you look at the bigger picture. And so what you actually have to do as a trainer when you do just drop in and out of communities is work along people's timelines that they have already set up. So having that group and a lot of people participating in that process allows for people to come and go, in and out where they can while still being open to train them along all the different stages.

ANNA CADDEN
WETT MEDIA TRAINER, 2009

work in a highly collaborative and respectful manner. They show respect for and interest in the language and culture of the learners, favour side by side delivery and do not judge the learners' performance.

In our research we observed that successful expert mentors invariably facilitated productive learning activities that were project-based, rather than assessment-driven, and built upon a sense of mutual respect, the development of real and ongoing relationships, recognition of learners' existing knowledge and repetition of key concepts. These principles apply particularly well to the learning of new digital technologies, as musician Chris Reid suggests with reference to the technical process of learning the *GarageBand*

EXPERT MENTORS WORKING WITH YOUNG PEOPLE

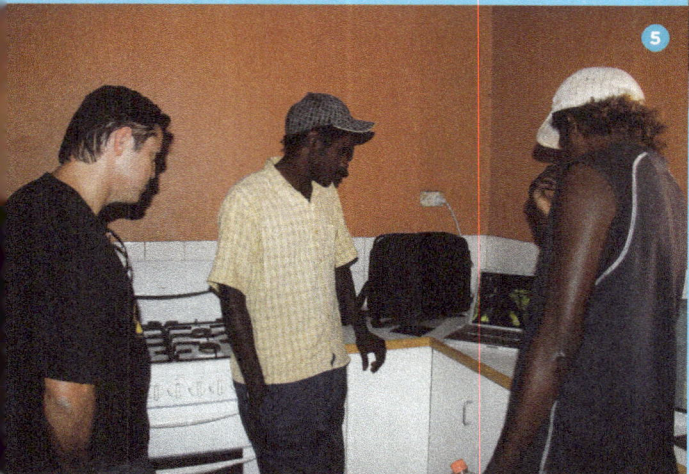

1. ANNA CADDEN WITH SHANE WHITE

2. MARGARET CAREW WITH GAYLE CAMPBELL

3. JANE LEONARD WITH BELINDA O'TOOLE AND SADIE RICHARDS

4. JASON GIBSON WITH MAXWELL TASMAN

5. DANIEL FEATHERSTONE WITH RICARDO WESTON AND AMOS URBAN

ALL PHOTOS: YOUTH LEARNING PROJECT

In addition to learning from 'expert mentors' or trainers from outside the community, in many of the projects we observed youth learning from older relatives and each other. Significantly, new digital technologies lend themselves to a process of peer to peer learning and it is important that this style of learning is facilitated and supported.

In the field of music, for example, *formal* training has rarely been an option in remote regions: the young have typically learned by imitating the styles of older musicians. As children they mimicked drum rhythms with their hands or played 'air guitar', and as adolescents they honed their focus through observation, listening, and experimentation (Kral 2011a). This is reflected in the *GarageBand* studio at Ngaanyatjarra Media where a three-tier hierarchy is often apparent: musicians in their mid-twenties such as Chris and Nathan, are the main singers, musicians,

music recording application from a mentor expert musician:

> He came out here and showed us this recording thing, *GarageBand* computer. Showed us that, said that we can record songs on here, easy way....and we started from there then. It was little bit hard when we first started...Once we got used to it, it was right then. Started recording. He showed us a couple of times, a couple of days then we was doing it all by ourselves...He just let us do it. If we make a mistake we'll call him then he'll come. Then he'll just help us, then he'll go. He'll let us off then and then when make another mistake we'll call him. Then he'll show us, he'll keep showing us until we catch it all, you know. That's a good way of learning. That's an easy way of learning, like when people show you, when you practice, like when you do it, when someone show you and you do it again, and you do it, and try again and you'll get it, you'll catch it, like that. The more you practice the more you learn, like that...we learn from making mistakes.

> I see more of the youngfellas are interested in music and some youngfellas that are now adult they're learning from young people, like how to use the *GarageBand*. So not only the teachers are showing the Anangus, teaching, it's like young people, like young Anangu fellas or *kungka*, like girl or boy, teaching others, teaching the older Anangus. 'Cause the older Anangus like they watch how the young people are doing and they get interested in that and they just ask, anytime, anyway, and they'll show them.
>
> **NATALIE O'TOOLE**
> WINGELLINA COMMUNITY, 2008

and producers; adolescents in their mid-teens are actively learning from these older musicians; and school-age children sit on the sidelines observing and imitating the memorised moves on instruments while recordings are replayed on the computer.[4] These 'intent participants' (Rogoff et al. 2003), or 'little young ones' as Chris calls them are not excluded or sent out of the room. Instead, they are incorporated, given space to observe, and occasionally offered the opportunity to try out a technique as part of an understood process of moving from observation to imitation. Instructional interactions are ad hoc and tend to be non-verbal, although on occasion an older 'mentor' may relay specific oral information to a junior 'apprentice'. This situation is echoed across the research sites. At Djilpin Arts a worker suggests that this form of 'peer training' works 'because they speak the same language, know the other kids and it's so much better that they are being trained by their own mob'.

DESIGN PRINCIPLE 4:
A SPACE TO GROW INTO NEW ROLES AND RESPONSIBILITIES

The kind of youth-oriented organisations outlined here provide opportunities for young adults to participate in project-based learning and take on responsible goal-oriented roles. Expert mentors and other enabling adults also play an important supporting role in keeping young people, who have been trained, engaged and actively involved in ongoing projects. Through playing a variety

> A lot of it comes down to having a strong goal. What you want to do and how you're gonna go about it. Once they see the steps to get there they take it on. But if there's no outcome or no goal, what point is there?
>
> MICAH WENITONG
> YOUTH WORKER, YUENDUMU, 2009

of adult roles that carry real consequences within a situation or organisation, young people take on meaningful roles and responsibilities and the process gives agency to the ideas of the participants.

Theatre work in particular is a context where youth participants assume meaningful roles. Through rehearsing, performing and touring around Australia with the *Ngapartji Ngapartji* theatre show the youth performers engaged in an intense, highly disciplined, rule-bound and physically demanding work routine. Performance 'work' was taken seriously. Ngapartji Ngapartji saw the potential in young people and expected them to perform at a high level. Young people had to learn the discipline of rehearsals and performance in a challenging learning space where every individual is expected to perform and shirking responsibility is not acceptable behaviour. In rehearsals they were assisted by the older *anangu* women who played an important role as mentors: they guided the young ones and repeated English stage directions in Pitjantjatjara. However once onstage, there was an expectation of unequivocal individual responsibility.

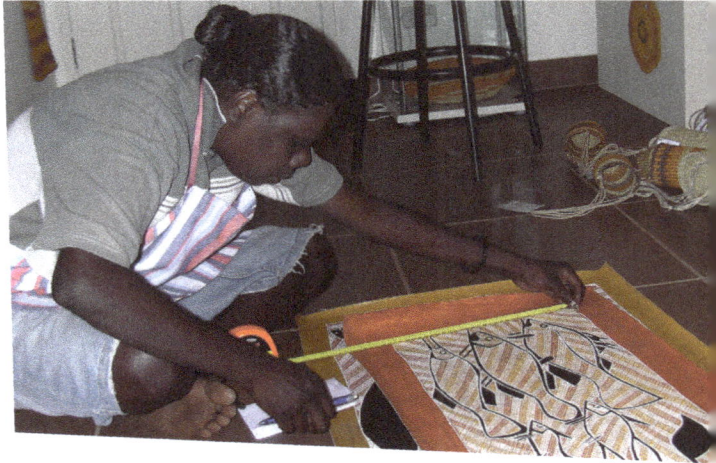

SCENARIO
NGAPARTJI NGAPARTJI
THEATRE PERFORMANCE,
SYDNEY, JANUARY 2008

Young people can be self-consumed and unco-operative, not concentrating on rehearsal instructions. In the rehearsal space they fiddle constantly with mobile phones and mp3 players. Until finally, these mobile devices are taken off them by the Director with much protestation by young people. Yet later the demand of the performance forces a level of concentration, listening, comprehending and reacting perfectly that is unlike everyday experience and unlike rehearsing. It is the performative moment, the real deal, like ceremonial performance.

Through touring young people learned the discipline of timetabled activities, routines, schedules and duties and responded positively as they had all chosen to be there. Young people were given real responsibilities, they were challenged to go the extra step in a risk-laden environment and they did. The progression from shyness to confidence was palpable. By stretching themselves beyond safe and familiar boundaries, young people recognised the need for a wider range of skills, including literacy.

Video-making also requires defined roles: a director, camera operator and editor. Sometimes they are the same person and sometimes they are different and young people gravitate to the roles that suit them. Editing of films on the computer is a long and arduous task, as Media Trainer Anna Cadden notes (interview 2009):

> Some young people have developed a real love for it. They have persisted in acquiring and practising the skills, turning up day after day at times when expert mentors have been running short workshops.

In video-making young people are experiencing control and ownership because they are the ones that know about the technology and new media. Oftentimes they are making cultural recordings with elders. Old people have clearly defined roles as the holders of cultural knowledge. Simultaneously young people are taking on language and culture maintenance roles as the facilitators of digital media. In this way media work is validated by elders who need young people to mediate between old knowledge and new technologies.

Media is a team activity, something that has a goal, it has an outcome that can then be shared with the whole community.

ANNA CADDEN
WETT MEDIA TRAINER, 2009

non-Indigenous alike. At the same time, young musicians are gaining status from having their recorded music listened to in the community, on local and national radio and uploaded to websites.[6]

Youth programs can also build up an understanding of what constitutes work, through encouraging responsibility and rewards for work. Interestingly, one youth centre had a lot of rules, mostly created by young people themselves to keep the space functioning. As a youth worker noted 'most of the rules are their rules and the rules have meaning for young people, unlike school rules.' Moreover the consequences for breaking rules make sense and this is allowing young people to take on individual responsibility in the communal space.

At Ngaanyatjarra Media as young people have acquired new skills they have taken on roles as producers, artists, song-writers, as well as musicians. Nathan quickly became known as the 'producer'. As a producer Nathan raises the bar and brings the other musicians up to a higher level. He wants to do music well, he teaches people, demonstrates his skill and others aspire to rise to that level.[5] Bands from communities hundreds of kilometers away would come over to the recording studio to have their songs recorded and produced by Nathan. These new local producers also train young people in their own and other communities. These young musicians work hard and take their roles seriously. They experience what it is to be driven, obsessed and connected to something that has cultural resonance and is valued by Indigenous and

We do have a lot of rules that we don't even realise, for example 'if the band doesn't pack up they don't get band the next day', 'if you're cooking you gotta clean up afterwards', 'no hand stands in the kitchen!' We got a 'no kids on the laptop' rule…It was actually a rule made by all the older kids. They said "Until those younger kids learn how to use that laptop they are not allowed on it!" So we're in the process of making a kids computer so they can delete what they want but still get that exposure…

AMY HARDIE
YOUTH WORKER, WILLOWRA, 2009

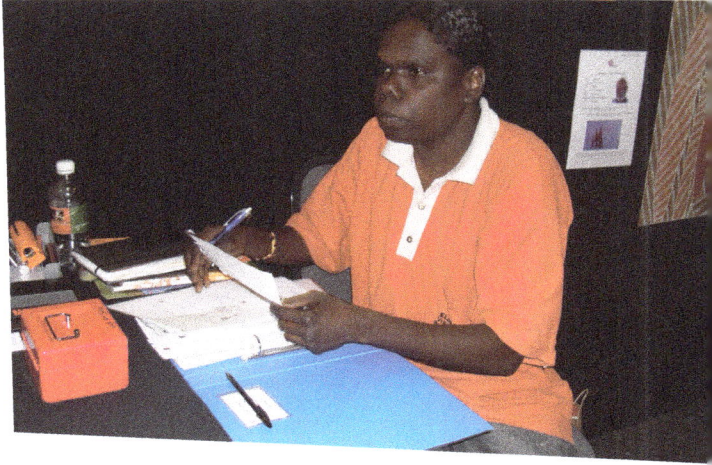

Djilpin Arts is community owned and controlled. This generates the sense that people have the right to own and participate in what is going on. In turn, this level of ownership carries obligations, and young people in particular are trusted with certain responsibilities, they work hard and they meet those responsibilities. Young people have to think about their participation and their ideas are taken seriously. Other community members see this, they see young women working in the Culture Centre having keys and responsibilities and they see young men being given responsibility for expensive camera equipment.

At the Culture Centre the young women want to understand what it takes to run the whole process and they want to do it themselves. If responsibility is given, they rise to it, moreover they embrace it. Revonna is the senior arts worker. She works full-time and is responsible, interested and committed. Significantly, Revonna has her own set of keys and every day she opens and closes the centre, a responsibility almost unheard of in most Aboriginal communities where non-Aboriginal people generally control the keys to community spaces. Importantly, it is assumed that Revonna is up to the task. As Revonna herself describes:

I have to check if everyone come to work at right time and make sure no-one's like, especially stranger, be near that office area, cause there's money anywhere inside, especially that phone money got to be kept in that little safe, that box. I'm trying to be careful like no-one go in because they might steal it. Also trying to make sure, like about that timesheet.

Revonna is aware that she has to demonstrate honesty, responsibility and leadership to the other young women because the shame of letting people down would be too great. The criteria for employment at the Culture Centre are not qualifications or literacy and numeracy competence, but familial networks and cultural authority. For Revonna the Culture Centre is 'a good place to work, to have culture and whiteman law at the same time'. It is this dimension that endows her with the cultural authority or 'right' to do the task at hand and she was employed on that basis and carries that responsibility. All the young women are given trust and they do not abuse it, they take responsibility for what they are doing with pride and this is reinforced by strong community support.

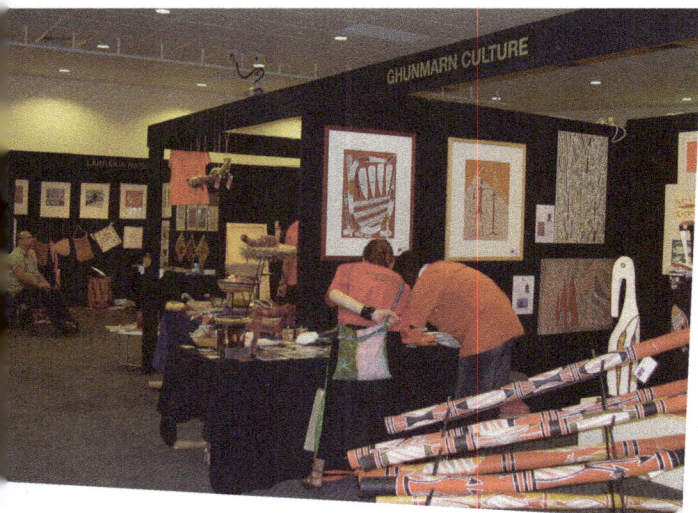

SCENARIO
AT THE CULTURE CENTRE

Revonna works full-time every day and takes responsibility for training three new girls who will work half day shifts from 9–12.30 and 12.30–4. At the end of every day the girls have to fill in a timesheet of hours worked. The young women work with Revonna to negotiate how they are going to work their shifts. They come up with the idea of making a roster. They all propose suggestions for how it should be done:

"I work usually from 12 to 4."

"Put it like this, do it sideways."

"Do them like this, rough one, and on computer neat one."

Revonna suggests laminating the roster so the names can be attached with blu-tac. They evaluate the suggestions and decide that this won't work. It is better that the same two girls work every morning shift and the other works every afternoon shift. That way they will remember who should be there, rather than use a written timetable.

They want to understand what it takes to run the whole thing, they want to do it themselves, they don't want to be bossed around forever. I think that they embrace the responsibility and the literacy and numeracy stuff doesn't seem to phase them. They'll check or go "Oh, I'm not sure"... there's heaps of things like that, just little things where you show them once and they know it. So they don't seem to struggle with the literacy and numeracy-based elements of their work as long as someone has shown them.

FLEUR PARRY
GENERAL MANAGER
DJILPIN ARTS, 2008

DESIGN PRINCIPLE 5:
A SPACE TO PRACTICE ORAL AND WRITTEN LANGUAGE

Earlier we noted the importance of youth engagement in collaborative tasks in youth-based organisations for language development. Heath and Street (2008: 99-100) note that the playing of meaningful roles 'ratchets up language performance' and 'supportive strict adult models who work alongside learners can provide language input that young learners pick up'. We found that where Indigenous youth are given responsibility for adult roles they seamlessly begin to engage in the performance and authentic practice of such roles. In many of the youth-oriented projects described here young people are given responsibility, assume production roles and collaborate with mentor experts who take them seriously and have high expectations of their performance. New forms of interaction with adults in the project sites are allowing young people to negotiate different types of social relations where they engage in complex turn-taking interactions with an expectation of high communicative competence. In the production roles outlined here, young people listen to cohesive stretches of technical discourse and participate in task-based and social exchanges in SAE. In these contexts young people acquire and practice genres and structures of English that are unfamiliar to them. In exchanges around participatory tasks, complex grammatical structures are modelled and repeated. Young people listen to and interpret instructions, request clarification and initiate ideas and actions in what is for many a

second language. In this mode of learning young people are also risk-takers when they push themselves forward to talk to non-Aboriginal people, as tour guides in arts centres or as performers on tour in urban centres.

Dani Powell, Assistant Director for the *Ngapartji Ngapartji* performance in Sydney in 2008 describes how, when young people are on tour, everyone is speaking in English 'so people have to work it out'. She states that in her role as Assistant Director a lot of time was spent translating what the Director was saying:

"What's he saying?" they ask.

And I reply: He says "We need the *company* to be stronger."

"What does *company* mean?" they ask.

Powell continues:

So learning the language of where we are and what's happening, and the need to know to be included, the need to know to get it right and not be shamed. I can't even count the number of times that people have asked me words, which hardly ever happens in town…But when we're travelling because you want to know if you can go in there or not, you want to know what the rules are, and I point that stuff out too so people start to realise: "Oh those signs are gonna help me get in and look good!"

Similarly, the young women who work at the Ghunmarn Culture Centre in Beswick learn customer relations skills and develop oral fluency and communication skills in SAE. Learning to be an arts worker requires interacting with other Indigenous and non-Indigenous workers, visitors and tourists and using SAE in a manner not typically encountered in everyday life. The arts workers code-switch between everyday discourse with each other in 'Kriol'[7] and SAE with non-Indigenous people. This entails using an informal register with familiars and a more formal speech register with visitors or tourists. It is linguistically and socially challenging for the young women to approach a group of non-Indigenous strangers and ask: "Would you like some help?". Likewise, making the shift from an informal register: "Can you smell it?" (referring to the soap they have made for sale) to the polite form "Would you like to smell it?", or from "You wanna look upstairs?" to "Would you like to look at the Blanasi Art Collection upstairs?", is demanding. It is through situated learning and practice that young people are enculturated into using these more formal registers.

The young women also have to be able to talk about the art, what it means, the language group of the artists and how it relates to the kinship system. Augustina Kennedy describes how she loves working at the Culture Centre 'because they've got my grandfather, great grandfather stories and painting'. Augustina has the cultural authority to show tourists the permanent Blanasi Collection where she tells her grandfather's story: 'I can remember and I always pass that

When tourists come I'm starting to push myself forward to talk in English really strongly and when they come to buy to something and I try to write it down and think, how do I start off first?...It's getting there to read, like by myself, like I kind of push myself to read more so I can get more better then.

REVONNA URBAN
BESWICK COMMUNITY, 2008

on' she tells visitors. She carries on the personal legacy of this inheritance. Augustina also has a special way of connecting with visitors and making them feel comfortable *because* she shares this personal connection when she talks about how some of the artworks were painted by her grandfather and great grandfather. Augustina appears to interact easily with the tourists because she intersperses English phrases of social etiquette such as "How was your morning?". Augustina is able to code-switch into SAE and deal with these linguistically demanding social situations. Nevertheless, she has to work hard at these oral interactions as English is not her first language.

At Beswick lack of literacy and numeracy is not a barrier to youth employment. All the young women who are arts workers have to learn computer skills and business skills, including cash flow implications and concepts of profit and loss. The young women must learn time management skills and remember the order and sequence of actions required to successfully operate the enterprise, all of which demand language, literacy and numeracy competence. In this way, they are gaining and practising the essential linguistic skills and organisational learning required of employees in any workplace.

In addition, in this Kriol-speaking community intergenerational exchanges offer a chance for young people to hear and practice their heritage languages (Rembarrnga, Dalibon, Mayali). The young women who work in the Ghunmarn Culture Centre collect sugar bag honey and plants with elders for the making of the beauty products and seek traditional language names and processes. In this process they assume a researcher role: collecting plant specimens, drawing information from elders, noting terms and seeking orthographical corrections from linguists. Elders collaborate with the young women to find plant names using published sources to compare plant specimens with drawings and photos. This activity generates community interest and people congregate. Young people ask questions and elders discuss the ways in which the plants were used in the old days, drawing on memories of traditional practices and linguistic forms.

In these environments the mother tongue is valued and cultural productions commonly incorporate oral or written texts in both the vernacular and English. These experiences are building positive identity formation and the development of the wide array of spoken and written forms needed for the multitude of intercultural, intergenerational situations which individuals experience daily and across the life course (Heath 1990; Heath 1997).

SCENARIO
GHUNMARN CULTURE CENTRE, BESWICK

A typical day's work for the young arts workers requiring oral and written communication skills, numeracy/business skills and cultural knowledge:

1. Welcome visitors.

2. Talk about the artists.

3. Describe how the work was made and the traditional uses of the objects.

4. Describe how the beauty products were made and the traditional uses of bush medicines.

5. Find or recall prices of objects.

6. Fill in sales sheets with catalogue numbers and codes, find certificates for artwork.

7. Add up prices correctly.

8. Ask customer if they want cash, savings or credit option. Use cash, EFTPOS or credit card facility correctly, give receipts and give the correct change.

9. Suggest or propose to visitors that they look at the 'Blanasi Art Collection' upstairs.

10. Make and serve coffee.

11. Catalogue new works coming in: measure canvases and price them according to what kind of work it is.

12. Prepare certificates to go with the work including the story for each piece, the artist's name, skin name, language group, and so forth.

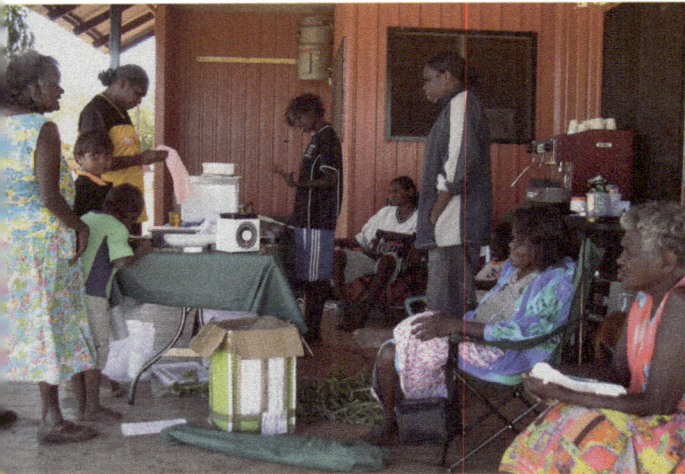

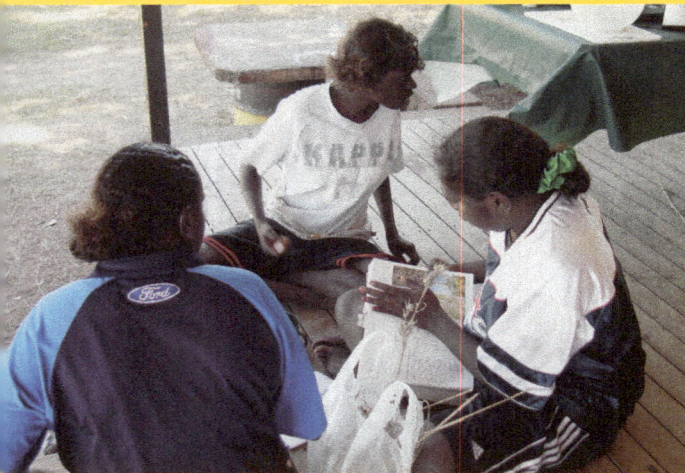

**YOUNG WOMEN RESEARCH BUSH PLANT NAMES
TO CREATE WRITTEN RESOURCES FOR BEAUTY
PRODUCTS SOLD AT GHUNMARN CULTURE CENTRE,
WUGULARR**

ALL PHOTOS: YOUTH LEARNING PROJECT

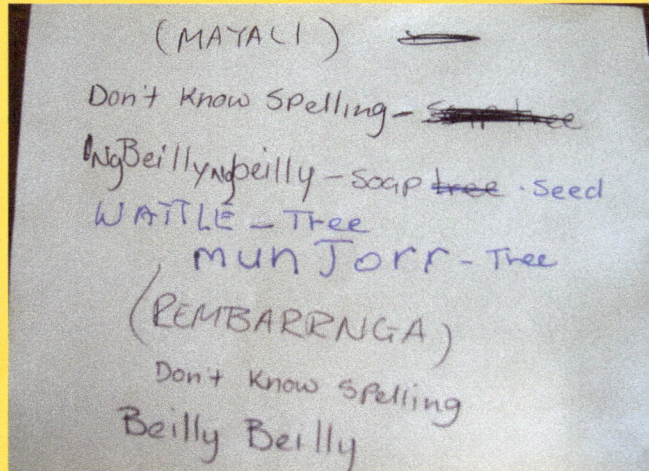

(MATACI)

Don't know Spelling — ~~Soap tree~~

NgBeilly ngbeilly — soap ~~tree~~ · seed

WATTLE — Tree

munJorr — Tree

(REMBARRNGA)

Don't know Spelling

Beilly Beilly

gU gU PRODUCTS

White Medicine Soap

CYMBOPOGON BOMBYCINUS
Family: Poaceae

Djirr or Jirr in Jawoyn

When you have a cough or flu you collect this
medicine grass and boil it up. You rub it on like
Vicks
Vaporub. It smells like lemon grass. Also you
can boil it up with water to make a wash for
scabies and skin sores.

Enjoy this soap – it will make your
skin clean and healthy!

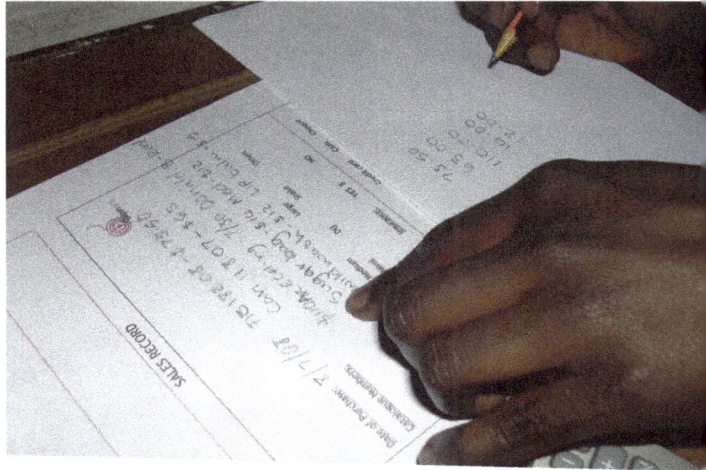

An important feature of learning spaces is their capacity to provide a place where adolescents and young adults can 'practice' their learning, including literacy. While this may be enabled just by having access to the resources needed for alphabetic or digital literacy activities, in some of the case studies we observed additional literacy support was provided.

The Ngapartji Ngapartji project employed literacy worker Jane Leonard to support young people's literacy development in integrated project-based activities. The young adult participants at Ngapartji are representative of the many Indigenous youth in remote regions who, says Jane, have 'slipped through the cracks' of current government strategies aiming at redressing poor engagement and outcomes in learning and literacy. All have English as a second, third or fourth language, attended school irregularly and had dropped out of school by Year 9. Consequently they have low English literacy levels. Additionally, they have had negative experiences of accredited adult literacy or training programs under current government legislation enforcing activity agreements as part of receiving Centrelink income support. Typically, they want to learn more but formal adult literacy courses are too confronting for them. Evidence from participants suggests that such courses have been intimidating, confusing, alienating, shaming, too hard, too easy, irrelevant, or a mixture of all these factors. Program objectives did not link to participant aspirations, needs, interests and skills, or provide any clear benefits. Consequently, participants did not attend or

dropped out—and were penalised financially. This cycle is often repeated over and over again, and perpetuates negative perceptions of the role of formal education. It also reinforces patterns of non-attendance and non-participation, as well as a sense of powerlessness and low self-esteem.[8]

While the youth participants possess low English literacy levels, these young people possess a range of competencies and aspirations.[9] The approach to learning taken by Ngapartji Ngapartji worked for them. They were able to maintain and develop their alphabetic literacy with the project-based literacy worker who engaged youth by merging media with intergenerational learning drawing on experiences of performance and production with the show, digital photo, videos and web-based productions. Literacy was enhanced because it was part of a situated and culturally meaningful activity. In the context of the Ngapartji Ngapartji project all the young people made significant contributions and achievements in arts, culture, language and multimedia forums and tangibly contributed to the success of a nationally recognised and critically acclaimed theatre project.

Best way to learn is to do it, get in there, get your hands dirty, get on there, play with it... Access can be a huge problem, one of the main things that can lead to success there. Anybody who is interested and wanting to learn through media needs access to a computer. Consistently doing stuff outside of school, as a lifestyle and as part of everyday life. People need access everyday...because of lack of infrastructure it's been difficult to gain access to these computers on a regular basis, every single day. Learning won't continue if people don't have access every day...

MICAH WENITONG
YOUTH WORKER, YUENDUMU, 2009

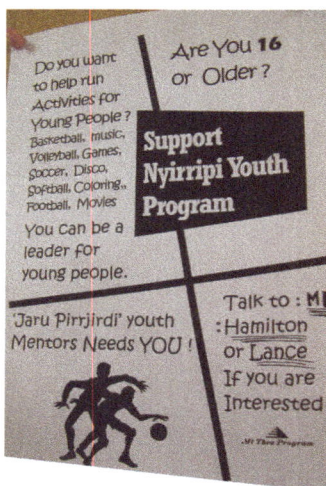

NYIRRIPI YOUTH CENTRE FLYER
PHOTO: YOUTH LEARNING PROJECT

In the past it was hard to get things rolling from scratch. Well spatially, physical space, there's been a BRACS room here but it hasn't been operational for a long time because there were questions over who was responsible for it and that caused a lot of problems with its upkeep and its maintenance and it wasn't looked after... it became a sort of unviable space in the community without people being willing to take responsibility for it. So that meant that that sort of space if you like was sort of out of bounds and not accessible to many people... Now there's a direct line from this very strong youth program and *Jaru Pirrjirdi* and all these other committees and activities are happening around the youth program. So now there's this quite clear through-line. There are people coming and engaging with media in a different way to where it's been before I think...Also with the youth programs being installed in communities now where there haven't been youth programs before, that also adds a massive support to media training, letting people have access to it on a regular basis...I think the whole vocational thing, whilst that's the point of the WETT training if you like, it's not what brings people to the training it's not why people come to learn video, it's because they want to learn video. Having that space where you could rock up every day—and people knew where you were and it was embedded in the community, right in the centre next to the shop.

ANNA CADDEN
WETT MEDIA TRAINER, 2009

Likewise the Mt Theo youth program at Yuendumu operated a Night School for young people wanting additional literacy support. Night School is an initiative from the *Jaru Pirrjirdi* (Strong Voices) Project. It came about when young adults expressed interest in furthering their education. Many of these young adults had left school early or had negative experiences within the institutional education and/or training system. Night School aimed to provide a less formal environment through which the young adults could re-access education. Importantly, this approach involved self-initiated learning

where young people shaped their own re-engagement with learning (often with school-like alphabetic literacy) according to their self-defined learning needs. There was no prescribed curriculum, but Night School activities involved creative and media rich experiences including mathematics, English, science, reading, writing, art, music, dance, and computers. Additionally, Night School opportunities were provided for young people to participate in practical workshops on issues including sexual health, substance misuse forums and dealing with 'government forms'.[10]

As these examples show, it is critical that we conceptualise literacy not only as a skill learned at school, but also as a competency acquired in situ without the need for formal lessons. Even without the provision of specific literacy tuition it is crucial that youth workers, arts workers and media trainers be mindful of creative ways to support participants with low level literacy. Suggestions for additional alphabetic literacy strategies in English and Aboriginal languages can be found in Appendix 2.

A lot of the online educational material that I've seen isn't very engaging it's pretty boring. And it's just the wrong way to approach to developing IT skills or digital literacies or whatever you want to call it amongst Aboriginal kids, it needs to be offline, face to face, in communities using resources that are available online but it needs to be once again a localized activity and supported in the local context. I think there's this attitude within some levels of government and other agencies that are saying let's develop online resources for people. But I know from my work with people in communities that's almost pointless because you need to be able to direct people to this stuff and they need to feel like they belong to it...I just think that that approach of let's develop online education isn't really, it's not there yet. That's not to say it won't happen in the future, but because of those barriers it's not really where we should be heading at the moment, I don't think.

JASON GIBSON
NTL MEDIA TRAINER, 2008

We've got Macs, PCs and the X-Box as well. Kids love burning CDs, it's the number one thing to do! Play lists on *iTunes*, photos, printing photos. When we first got here I was amazed by some of the computer skills. Like something would break on a Mac and we'd leave it with M. or someone and come back ten minutes later and she'd have fixed it! I'd have spent an hour on it and couldn't get past how to open it up. I'm sure there's a lot of literacy skills that they are learning without even realising it...Because most of the kids don't go to school after 12 or 13, anything they do is really good. In doing stuff they ask you how to spell something. Just basic, but for them they quite enjoy it, goes at their own pace, they do what they want. And it's better because they are doing it because they want to do it, rather than because they are told to.

KYLE JARVIE
YOUTH WORKER, WILLOWRA, 2009

LANA CAMPBELL, TI TREE
PHOTO: YOUTH LEARNING PROJECT

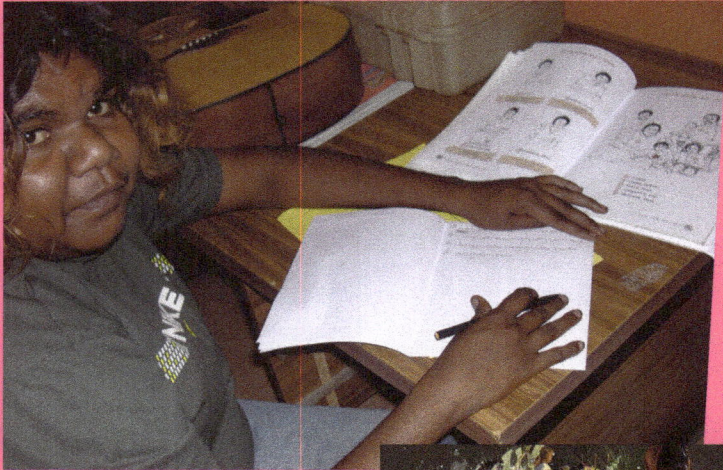

SADIE RICHARDS,
NGAPARTJI NGAPARTJI
PHOTO: YOUTH
LEARNING PROJECT

NGAPARTJI NGAPARTJI WEBSITE
©NGAPARTJI NGAPARTJI

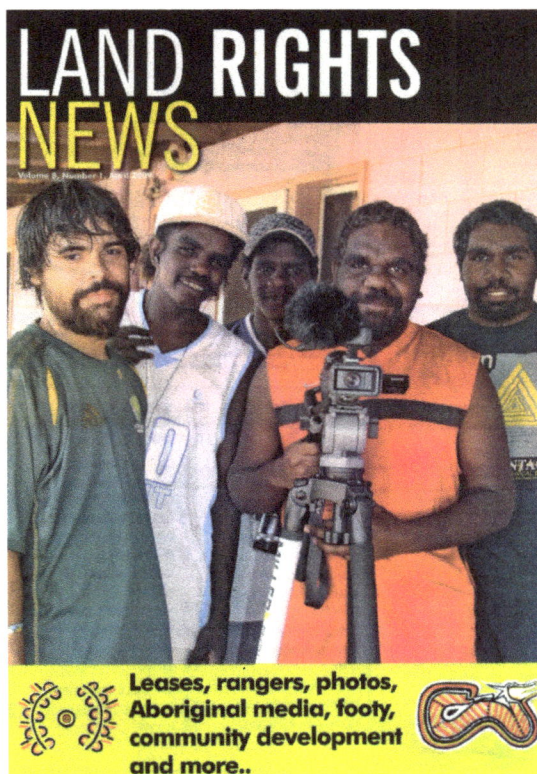

DESIGN PRINCIPLE 6:
A SPACE TO EXPRESS SELF AND CULTURAL IDENTITY THROUGH MULTIMODAL FORMS

Theorists (Gee 2003; Kress 2003) have called on policymakers to reflect and rethink how we consider communication, literacy and learning in these new economic, social and technological times. In the Indigenous arena we see little evidence of innovative thinking or reasoned challenges to old conceptions of literacy, as policy makers and education department bureaucrats tend to come from the pre-digital age group. Commentators often assume a shared understanding of what literacy is, yet few have moved beyond a school-based deficit perspective on alphabetic literacy and so often appear not to notice the changing modes of literacy in the 'new media age' (Kress 2003).

As we have outlined, in the various research sites for this project young people are experiencing self-directed, creative, meaningful productive activity enabled by access to resources and a sense of spatial control. We also suggest that concurrent with the penetration of computers, mobile phones and online social networking in remote communities, alphabetic and digital literacy strategies are being used to create unique, culturally meaningful products. Accordingly, we are beginning to see how digital technology is transforming modes of oral and written communication in the remote Indigenous context. With access to resources and regular practice, new forms of textual communication

and linguistic creativity are emerging. Here multimodal practice is reliant on standardised alphabetic symbols coupled with left to right and top to bottom processing; simultaneously it is interacting with a pictographic symbol system to provide a new communicative repertoire. Indigenous young people, like their peers in urban Australia and overseas, are constructing and framing multimodal texts using intertextual layering of image, text, song and gesture (Hull 2003; Ito et al. 2010). Importantly, it is evident that where young people have access to digital resources and technologies they are engaging in new forms of media production to express themselves and their cultures. In doing so they are incorporating a range of multimodal literacies (encompassing oral, written, visual, and gestural modes of representation and communication).

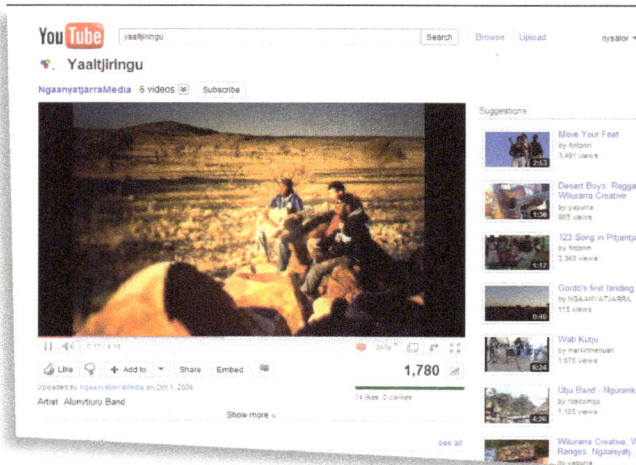

Indigenous youth are also using digital technologies and alphabetic text in the maintenance of social relationships and the generation of new cultural products. In media centres, LKCs and even in homes in communities with mobile phone or Wi-Fi internet access, youth are uploading personal profiles, photos and films, using text and symbols in inventive ways, and writing—usually in English—about themselves and to each other. Through *Facebook* and mobile phone text messaging they are maintaining sociality and stretching the boundaries of what is possible, including transferring mobile phone photos and film to *Facebook*, reformatting films to bluetooth between mobile phones, and dragging sound files from digital heritage archives onto mp3 players.[11]

> When we make a song we just get a pen and a paper then write the song down, write the meaning and all that, right meaning. We make sure if it's right, correct spelling and all that... Then we check it, make sure if it's right, then we put it on, record it. We record it on the computer, first we make the song right then we sing it. You press the red button that says record, press that. Then you record the voice. Then after when you finish you press stop. Then you can go back and listen to it. Press play. That's recorded there and you just listen to it. We'll practice a couple of times before we put it on, before we record it. If we're not happy we just leave it there or sometimes we just put it in the trash, just that track. Song, whole song sometimes or track.
>
> **CHRIS REID**
> WINGELLINA COMMUNITY, 2008

Multimedia productions provide insights into how Indigenous youth are symbolising and expressing their shared experiences and practices as a generational cohort. The visual, creative nature of multimedia work illuminates the cultural practices and symbol structures in image and language that young people are using for identity formation. Openly displayed are the systems of cultural meaning that shape their awareness. Multiple meanings are embedded in the language used by young people. Through the incorporation of intercultural elements young people are forming 'semiotic reconstructions' (Pennycook 2003: 527) and forging new cultural identities, perspectives and understandings. They are challenging stereotypes and creating less bounded constructs of Aboriginality. Through their use of dress, gesture, visual symbolism and performative modes in their representations of individual or group identity, young people are not replicating the past, but creating new forms.

Song composition represents perhaps the most pertinent example of contemporary forms of youth engagement with oral and written texts in the post-school years. Songs recorded by the musicians on *GarageBand* are transcribed and translated from the vernacular to English as text for CD covers by those with the literacy skills,

Well with my husband I help him write in Pitjantjatjara and in English...because I can write faster than him, well that's how I see it! And like, I'm like a teacher to him, but he can read and write in English and he can read in Pitjantjatjara, but only little bit of writing, yeah. 'Cause in Wingellina it's mixed up, it's in Western Australia but they speaking Pitjantjatjara. Some talking Ngaanyatjarra 'cause they from Ngaanyatjarra Land.

NATALIE O'TOOLE
WINGELLINA COMMUNITY, 2008

generating pride in Aboriginal language and identity. Natalie O'Toole is literate in English and Pitjantjatjara. She has assisted with transcribing and translating the songs for the *Alunytjuru Band* CDs. She uses *iTunes* to create a playlist of the songs. She listens to each song, transcribes it and then translates it, checking the Pitjantjatjara-English Dictionary as she goes.

The content of songs (and other texts including films) produced by remote youth form a repertoire of persistent and predictable Aboriginal themes (such as mobility and looking after kin and country). Songs produced by young people at Wingellina provide insights into how they are reflecting on current circumstances and, moreover, visualising and constructing a positive sense of self, projecting pride in their linguistic and cultural identity and taking responsibility for looking after the land inherited from their elders. As Chris and Nathan explain:

> Music is our way to give a strong message...looking after our sacred areas and waterholes and grandfathers' land, that's a strong message, like so younger generation can see that, and listen to that, and understand what the message is.

At Ngaanyatjarra Media young musicians are merging the intercultural elements of Indigenous language, gesture and style with global youth culture and English, thus forging and expressing new cultural perspectives, understandings and identities. In this way we are witnessing a blend of cultural continuity, innovation and transformation across the generations. Moreover, enterprise is being generated out of the young people's connection to kin and country and their responsibility to look after the land.

Ngura Alunytjuru
(Our country Alunytjuru)

Long time ago when I was young my grandfather showed me the places
I still remember the Dreamtime waterhole he showed me in the past
What a beautiful place to get the water from, Alunytjuru-la
What a beautiful place he showed me, I'll never forget[12]

Anangu tjuta
(All the people)

Anangu tjuta kukaku ananyi putiku kukaku.
Anangu tjuta kurunpa pukulpa wirura ngurangka.
Manta wirunya ngayuku.
Nganampa ngura wirunya.
Anangu tjuta ngurangka nyinanyi.
Tjukurpa putitja nintini.
Kamilu, tjamulu manta ungkutja ngananganya wirura.

All the people going hunting out bush for meat.
All the people their spirit is alive happily at home.
My land is beautiful.
Our home is beautiful.
All the people at home teaching bush stories.
Our grandparents gave this land to us to look after.[13]

DESIGN PRINCIPLE 7:
A SPACE TO DEVELOP AND ENGAGE IN ENTERPRISE

In the research sites we found successful economic enterprises generated by youth and the community themselves, often around shared cultural belief systems where both material and 'symbolic' production (Bourdieu 1984) is valued. Indigenous cultural connection is at the core of many enterprise ventures. The cultural values that determine youth aspirations are inclusive of caring for kin and country and transmitting knowledge to the next generation. Where activities are tied to meaningful community projects, we are seeing youth engaging as the mediators and facilitators of cultural productions in collaborative, intergenerational activities that positively affirm their contemporary Indigenous identity.

Djilpin Arts is unique in that it emphasises both youth learning and enterprise development as priority areas. Typically, Aboriginal arts centres in remote Australia bring in specialists from outside to run their centres. Djilpin Arts is an Aboriginal organisation and the community wants real ownership of the centre, which means employing local people and providing local enterprise options and pathways. The main enterprise focus is the Culture Centre, a pivotal social and cultural site where there is activity and a sense of things happening. Older people are the traditional artists and artefact makers. They can sell their work to the Culture Centre and receive an immediate cash payment, whereas young adults have few of these skills. Finding

Soap Wild sugar bag soap is a clear honey coloured oval with tiny balls of the invaluable dark brown wax embedded in it. Both gugu and the wax have antiseptic qualities and are valued by indigenous people for their healing properties. The soaps are rich in glycerine which scavenges moisture from the air and delivers it to your skin. Sometimes, in periods of high humidity the soap collects more moisture than it can store. Tiny bubbles can form on the surface of the soap, they should not be wiped away as they will reabsorb into the soap when the weather dries off.

Balm Wild sugar bag lip balm is deliciously perfumed with the sweet lemon scented gugu. You won't find this special flavour anywhere else on earth. The luscious aromas and flavours are carried in gentle moisturizing oils which leave your lips sensually protected from the harsh Australian climate.

Candles Wild sugar bag candles carry the scent of the wax and honey, so you can take some wild essential Arnhemland into your home anywhere in the world.

Gugu Premium pure wild gugu is 100% wild honey. It is rich and delicious. The flavour can vary from one batch to the next because each hive is dependent upon seasonal wild blossoms. Traditionally eaten by dipping a grass stick into the honey, or try dabbing it on the back of your hand and licking it off. Like perfume, the warmth of your skin will bring out the aromatic esters locked into the honey. Use this wild product sparingly.

enterprise-generating activities for young people is an economic necessity. At the Ghunmarn Culture Centre enterprise and employment are generated out of young people's connection to kin, country and traditional practices. There are insufficient arts worker positions for the number of young women requesting employment, so a café and beauty products enterprise (making soap, lip balm and candles out of natural bush medicines and plants) has been established as an income generating project for young people. Augustina works part-time at the culture centre and supplements her income making beauty products:

I was learning about that soap, bush honey soap, candles...When tourists come to buy something I learn about that and I've learned about how to sell soap. I know how you use computer, EFTPOS, and I know how to write down catalogue, when they buy something what number go on and write that down. I wanna keep working here.

The marketing of the beauty products is aimed at satiating a European Australian market for 'authentic' Indigenous products and the young women are well able to deliver products to meet the market requirements for quality and presentation. Here young women have a modern role that connects them with the knowledge of the past. Hence they have agency in the production of beauty products that are both modern and attractive to tourists, *and* meaningful within the local context. They, like the young filmmakers, music producers, festival organisers and oral historians, have developed skills that are of recognised value and can in many cases generate an income.

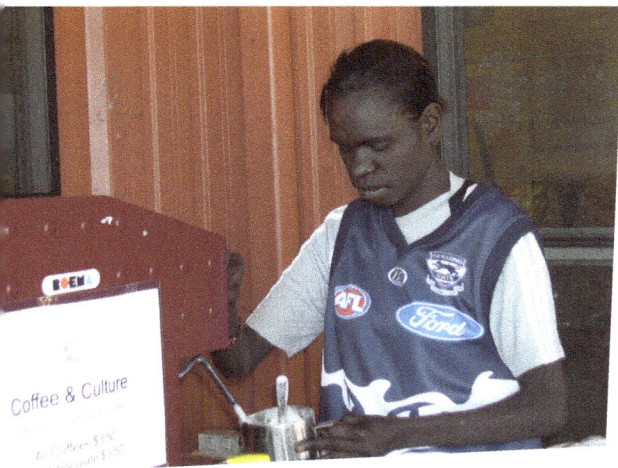

AUGUSTINA KENNEDY MAKING COFFEE AT GHUNMARN CULTURE CENTRE
PHOTO: YOUTH LEARNING PROJECT

DESIGN PRINCIPLE 8
A SPACE TO ENGAGE WITH THE WORLD

Throughout this book our interpretation of the context and the findings has been shaped by our anthropological orientation. From this perspective it is impossible to ignore the reality that for many remote youth a close and meaningful relationship with the traditional past has been maintained. It has been suggested (Brooks 2011) that the Ngaanyatjarra and other Western Desert groups share a world of meaning that derives from the *tjukurrpa* (the 'Dreaming') and this is still manifest in the way in which they interpret many aspects of the world. Moreover, irrespective of their contemporary demeanour, Western Desert youth have imbibed this world view from their elders and maintain an underlying cultural propensity for what Brooks (2011) calls '*tjukurrpa*-thinking' in everyday life. Such a worldview is present in each of the sites in which we worked. Simultaneously, however, these young people are immersed in the 'global cultural flow' (Appadurai 1996).

The young people we have worked with and have described in this book are not rejecting culture. Access to elders and traditional knowledge remains a vital part of what matters to them. Rather, they are seeking new ways of expressing a contemporary Indigenous identity. They are change agents, drawing on pre-existing knowledge and skills drawn from being members of the local community, but also seeking to know more about the outside world. They are mediating between old knowledge and new

technologies and creating contemporary forms of cultural production. Through music, theatre, film and various social media, Indigenous youth are engaging with the world. Through these means they showcase their skills and creations and cultures. There is always some element of risk in opening new doors, but young people appear to discount that risk in their desire to tell their stories, to communicate and learn. Their experience is one in which their own culture is preserved and celebrated, yet they actively and consciously engage with the world in a way their grandparents could never have envisaged. Accordingly, their entry into learning spaces and their engagement with productive learning is at once transformative and affirming.

In addition, productions by youth are helping to counter negative public perceptions associated with Indigenous youth in remote communities. Writing and production *by youth* rather than *about youth* provide insights into how these young people are reflecting on their circumstances, projecting their futures and developing their own style. Importantly they indicate that young people are visualising and constructing a positive sense of self (Bauman and Briggs 1990). Gaining control of the technology and being able to manipulate the medium and the images themselves means that there is no longer 'some outsider recording them', so young people are in control of their own self-representation. Interestingly, many productions by youth (writing, images, films, songs) developed independently or with peers, with little adult or non-Aboriginal direction or intervention, tend to express a humorous, joyful, love of life and validate who they are. As Anna Cadden (Interview 2009) notes:

I think so much of the media attention and films and docos, everything that is made *about* remote communities is always hard line, strong messages. Whereas you look at films made from the community and it's this joy of life sort of stuff.

Wider viewings of films online and at festivals or conferences are allowing young people to position themselves as productive contributors in the national and international domain. As we have mentioned, young people are uploading productions to websites such as *YouTube* and alerting each other on *Facebook*. In addition community-generated media productions are broadcast as free to air local community broadcasts, or on ICTV and IndigiTube, as well as the Remote Indigenous Media Organisations (RIMOs) and their websites.[14] The majority of films and videos produced by remote youth are in local Indigenous vernacular/s and incorporate translated subtitles in English. Such productions are an important vehicle for language and culture revival, maintenance and transmission. While some national platforms exist for the broadcasting of youth productions in local languages (e.g. through NITV; ABC Open; and Yarning Up), there remains a strong need for local community broadcasting services such as ICTV (Rennie and Featherstone 2008).

> The festival is fun, everybody dances, everybody works, everybody's involved in it... They hang out there, everybody hangs out there. If we run some kind of music workshop with the old guys on the veranda of the red house there'll be 20 young guys coming around hanging out to be part of it.
>
> **FLEUR PARRY**
> GENERAL MANAGER
> DJILPIN ARTS, 2008

Festivals such as the biannual *Milpirri Festival* at Lajamanu, the annual *Walking with Spirits Festival* at Beswick, the *Turlku Purtingkatja* music festivals in the Ngaanyatjarra Lands, the *Bush Bands Bash* in Alice Springs or the annual Remote Media Festivals[15] provide opportunities to consolidate the intergenerational connection between performance, cultural tradition and community wellbeing. These events are sites for the regeneration of a strong cultural identity and offer a rare chance for collaboration and exchange between Indigenous and non-Indigenous participants.

The *Walking with Spirits Festival,* for example, deftly weaves together culture, performance and enterprise. A high profile regional event, it blends the intergenerational transfer of Indigenous tradition and the cross-cultural sharing of music, dance and visual and material arts. Over the Festival weekend in August 2009, some 200 visitors passed through the Cultural Centre where the sale of art and coffees generated significant income. Augustina worked on the coffee machine in the outside cafe both days, while Revonna worked inside the Culture Centre talking to visitors and selling art: taking cash, EFTPOS or credit cards, giving change and receipts, printing out certificates and packing artwork. In the evening all the young people worked on the festival helping backstage and showed their recent media productions.

Festivals provide an opportunity for young people to set their minds to producing music or theatre performances or films. Often this is innovative work that will showcase their skills. Such events incorporate an element of risk. It is at festivals that young people are able to display performances that are representative of continuity, transformation and innovation and these performances are celebrated by all and affirm a contemporary Indigenous identity.[16] Importantly, all these settings provide a space for young people to express their contemporary Indigenous identity and engage with the world on their own terms.

As we mentioned at the beginning of this volume, the potential of Indigenous youth in remote Australia and the projects they engage in often lies unacknowledged. In the final section of this book we draw some conclusions and discuss how to better support youth learning and sustainable outcomes for successful optimistic futures in remote Australia.

Chapter 4 endnotes

1. Jane Leonard, pers. comm., June 2008.

2. The relationship between public libraries, youth development and lifelong learning has been established in the United States (Rothbauer et al. 2011).

3. See Kral (2012).

4. The new recording studio at the Wilurarra Creative youth arts project in Warburton is also a multigenerational site. Older musicians transfer cultural authority and rights over their song recordings to emerging artists, and work with the technical expertise of the younger generation to record music in the digital environment, while children hover on the periphery developing their musical skills through observation and imitation (Kral 2011a).

5. Daniel Featherstone, pers. comm., June 2009.

6. http://www.youtube.com/watch?v=Fd4pQaRa9EI&feature=related

7. The lingua franca for the region is the English-based creole known as 'Roper River Kriol' (Sandefur 1979).

8. Jane Leonard, pers. comm., June 2008.

9. Assessments made by Inge Kral in collaboration with Ngapartji Ngapartji using *The National Reporting System* (Coates et al. 1995) as an assessment tool.

10. *Yapa-kurlangu Yimi*. Mt Theo-Yuendumu Substance Misuse Aboriginal Corporation December 2006 Newsletter.

11. Jason Gibson, pers. comm., March 2008.

12. Lyrics: Chris Reid and Nathan Brown. © Alunytjuru Band 'Wati Kutju', Ngaanyatjarra Media.

13. Lyrics: Rosaria Scales. Singers: Hinerangi Tukere, Natalie O'Toole and Rosaria Scales. © Turlku 3, Ngaanyatjarra Media.

14. See ICTV: http://www.ictv.net.au/ and internet sites: http://www.indigitube.com.au/, http://www.pawmedia.com.au/, http://www.djilpinarts.org.au/digital/index.html

15. http://remotemedia.wikispaces.com/FESTIVAL+2011

16. See Handleman (1990) for a discussion on the role of public events and performances for skills development in young people.

CHAPTER 5

YOUTH, LITERACY AND LEARNING SPACES

In this final chapter we summarise the main findings of our research and suggest ways in which communities, practitioners and policy makers can support learning and literacy in remote Indigenous communities.

This book has reported on findings emerging from our efforts to answer three central research questions.

▸ How can early school leavers and disaffected young adults in remote communities be re-engaged with learning?

▸ How can literacy be acquired, maintained and transmitted outside school settings?

▸ How can learning and literacy be fostered across the lifespan?

Our search for answers to these questions involved a rich and productive collaboration with a range of Indigenous young people from remote communities, many of whom were themselves concerned with these questions. That collaboration resulted in an ethnographic study of learning, highlighting the many ways in which these and many other young people are developing the linguistic and conceptual skills and competencies (including language and literacy), technological know-how, and the work-oriented habits and attitudes required to move towards responsible adult roles and to function as competent members of their own and other communities. Importantly, this was all taking place outside of institutional education

settings. As highlighted in this book, this search also involved an exploration of an international theoretical literature that helped make sense of what we were observing and documenting and to draw on the insights that have emerged from research among other young people around the world.

Essentially, all three of our original questions are variations on the question: 'how can learning and literacy be supported in remote Indigenous communities?' We believe there is no more important question than this one. Our intention with this volume has not been to critique schooling and adult training, but rather to start a discussion that sheds light on the importance of 'non-formal' learning spaces. While we wish to emphasise again that our goal has not been to find a replicable or prescriptive model or method, we have in the chapters above identified what we believe are a starting set of principles for supporting productive learning activities. We hope these will be of value to individuals, communities and government when they are investing ideas and resources in supporting young people. In the summary we provide below we argue that these investments should emphasise three areas:

1. Supporting learning spaces.

2. Sustaining the local and creating links to the global.

3. Valuing a wide range of outcomes.

SUPPORTING LEARNING SPACES

The outcomes of this research project have shed light on the generative capacity of new digital technologies and how they are enabling linguistic creativity and new multimodal forms among the youth generation in remote Indigenous communities. On another level the findings from this project have provided insights into what is happening in this relatively invisible domain and how new learning spaces have developed leading to creative cultural production and enterprise activities. The findings have also illuminated other more subtle aspects. In these new learning spaces young people are learning at their own pace and in the process acquiring the experiences, skills and capacities that underpin their development as future community leaders. Moreover what is evident is that the content of these new forms of cultural production pivot around young people's ongoing connection to kin and country.

Our research shows that it is critically important that young adults have access to learning spaces where they have control over the physical space, and the time and the resources to acquire and practice relevant, new skills essential for productive activity. As we have seen, this control is often a precursor to adopting or acquiring meaningful community roles and responsibilities which are essential for young people as they embark on a path towards employment and enterprise and ultimately community leadership (see Figure 2).

FIGURE 2.
THE PROCESS OF PRODUCTIVE LEARNING

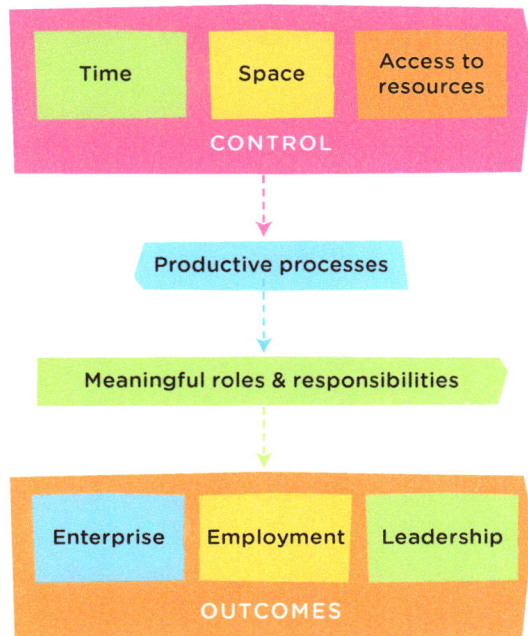

The productive learning facilitated by learning spaces involves a three-phase activity cycle:

1. Early phase trial and error experimentation and exploration.

2. Project-based learning often with mentor experts leading to intensive goal-oriented skills acquisition and interest-driven engagement.

3. Voluntary expertise development and independent creative cultural production leading to employment, enterprise and leadership.

We suggest that this activity cycle, and the embedded essential project-based learning approach, suits the remote youth learning context. The existence of a vibrant learning environment multiplies opportunities for engagement across and beyond the local community, and nurtures the development of enterprise, employment and leadership possibilities. While we acknowledge that mainstream education and accredited training works for some young people, there is clearly a significant number of adolescents and young adults who have enormous capacity and potential who are seeking other options for learning and meaningful activity. Many of the learning spaces we observed provide those options.

In summary, the processes of productive learning we observed in the learning spaces involved young people who are:

▶ experiencing meaningful participation in something that matters to them;

▶ thriving on trust and responsibility;

▶ learning individually or collaboratively as peers, yet able to call on mentors who offer advice or guide them toward the acquisition of new skills;

▶ increasing their skills and knowledge through practice, trial and error and learning from their mistakes;

▶ exerting a sense of control over what they are producing and how they are producing it;

▶ producing knowledge in the context of new and transformative processes;

▶ experimenting fearlessly; and

▶ visualising and achieving their desired goals.

Nevertheless, the achievement of productive learning is predicated on the alignment of a number of other elements. First, the community must value the program and have a sense of ownership; at the same time the non-Indigenous staff must be willing to share responsibility with the community, including handing over the keys (literally and metaphorically) to the learning space. Second, the community must participate in the development of clear guidelines around access to and the use of the technologies and facilities. Importantly, those guidelines must be supported and reinforced by the young people

similarly, the building of long-term productive relationships with the mentor experts who facilitate this growth requires flexibility and time. Recurrent funding models are the best means for supporting productive learning because they enable more flexible ongoing or customised sporadic training which takes into account locally-situated long-term needs and goals.

SUSTAINING THE LOCAL AND CREATING LINKS TO THE GLOBAL

Public discourse promotes the transition from school to training to employment in the 'real economy' (Pearson 2000) as the singular pathway to realising future opportunities for remote Indigenous youth. While mainstream employment is a pathway destination for some, for most it is not. Our research reveals weak linkages between schooling, training and employment in remote communities, and suggests that intergenerational models are not sufficiently robust for Indigenous youth to aspire to employment in the 'real economy'. Most importantly our findings indicate that many young people in remote communities do not imagine themselves leaving their community to seek employment. For them their responsibilities and their future lies at home, in 'belongingness' and in participation in meaningful, productive activities that will enhance the social and economic viability of their own communities.

(and their families) who use those facilities. Third, ongoing support for training, production and the maintenance of equipment is essential. Securing equipment and other large assets is sometimes relatively easy through one-off capital equipment funding programs, but without ongoing support those assets can become a liability. Specifically, in regard to training, a non-formal, project-based approach appears to be the most successful means for facilitating learning and skill acquisition. In particular, the approach allows for short, intense bursts of training by a visiting expert mentor. Such expert mentors play an essential supporting role in facilitating learning and keeping young people engaged and actively involved in ongoing projects. The best of these mentors actively pass on their skills to community members so that eventually their role is inhabited by a local expert. Obviously, while a traditional semester-based training delivery model suits annual bureaucratic funding rounds, it is too often inflexible and not conducive to maintaining participant engagement. It takes time for adolescents to pass through an initial 'entertainment and diversion' stage and to reach a point where they have acquired the skills and confidence for self-initiated productive activity;

An alternative vision in the Indigenous policy literature suggests another pathway for some Indigenous young people in remote areas through participation in the local 'cultural

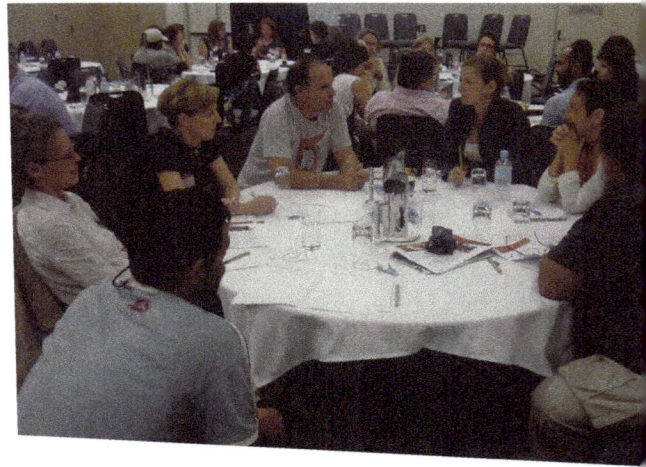

economy' or 'hybrid economy' (Altman 2007). This pathway, which involves engagement with and maintenance of local culture, may have more relevance, and thus more traction, than a trajectory of credentialisation that promises yet often fails to deliver abstract future employment outcomes away from home. Such an approach may be more successful in building the local economy, affirming Indigenous identity and thus providing a template of meaningful adult engagement for the next generation to replicate.

While our research revealed that learning was virtually never regarded as a means to an employment end, we have seen evidence that engagement with out-of-school productive learning can result in enterprise generation and employment. In this sense, economic outcomes are being achieved in the various sites, although not in accordance with the school-training-work model that most policy makers imagine. Youth employment opportunities are opening up in arts and cultural centres, in media and music production, and in the application of digital media skills to archival databases and 'working on country' projects. These economic enterprises pivot around shared cultural belief systems and semiotic resources where both material *and* symbolic production is valued. In this way we are seeing remote Indigenous youth drawing from the traditional Aboriginal context to become knowledge producers, but in transformed processes, by making the connection between the local community context and a contemporary market economy. Furthermore, while we have seen that many young people have an enduring desire to fulfil their responsibilities to kin and

country, they are relishing the opportunity to take up new tools and technologies which can help them to both fulfil those obligations and to engage with the outside world. While most see their futures in local terms, they also revel in the opportunities they have to share their culture and stories with the outside world.

The projects outlined in the preceding chapters work because they draw on Aboriginal language and culture and link closely with local community interests and needs. We have shown the intergenerational links and how the cultural work of youth is supported by elders. We emphasise this aspect as a counterpoint to negative media commentary by indicating the importance of these sorts of programs and projects for strengthening the fabric of remote Indigenous communities.

The young people who appear in this book are deeply committed to the future. The path they have chosen involves sustaining the local and creating links with the global. Achieving this will entail paying attention to learning environments outside instructional settings and finding pathways to productive learning that encourage language and multimodal literacy development,

I don't like to go in other places because I love it here and it's the way we growed up.

AUGUSTINA KENNEDY
BESWICK COMMUNITY, 2008

One young man rarely attended school, on the occasion when he did go he was often told by teachers to go away because he was too disruptive. One year he had a really good teacher and attended a few times that year. One day he went and they had a maths competition and he won the maths prize! Now he is working as professional cinematographer...He had aimlessness, but not now, now he works for a pretty good hourly rate in a highly skilled profession, which if he did want to keep going and go and work in the film industry that's a possibility for him but that's not the sole purpose of the program. It's not about skilling people up to send them out of the community because that doesn't work for most of the kids that I've seen. It's about saying that with these skills you can find the ways that they will be useful in your own community, it's about community viability.

FLEUR PARRY
GENERAL MANAGER
DJILPIN ARTS, 2008

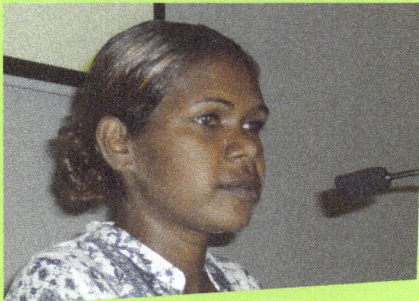

When I finished school ... I was still doing like helping each other, helping families and friends, ... I wasn't interested in AnTEP because for me it was like going back to school, ... I wanted to do my way, ... I was doing a little bit of teaching at the school, like reading books to little kids in English and Pitjantjatjara... People around me ... wanted me to work or do some things that sound good to them, but I didn't listen to them 'cause I didn't want people to force me, ... people forcing me it's like telling me to follow their footprints ...people shouldn't force people, ... because where I'll end up, I'll still end up a good life, ...Well for me, for the future, I would like to stay in *Anangu* community.

NATALIE O'TOOLE
PRESENTATION—
YOUTH LEARNING SYMPOSIUM
DARWIN, 2009

First learning is for yourself to be strong, before you can help others... All I can tell the government is strengthen the people first, let them choose whether they want to become a plumber or a lawyer or become a pilot, let them choose. All they got to take is right way teaching, really teaching for something, not just to look good...So I'm thinking, go back to the drawing board, go and make yourself strong first. That'll teach you everything about being a good parents too. That's what my culture taught me.

STEVE JAMPIJINPA PATRICK
WARLPIRI EDUCATOR AND LEADER
LAJAMANU, 2008

VALUING A WIDE RANGE OF OUTCOMES

A key feature of literacy and learning among Indigenous youth in remote Australia today is their adoption of, and intense engagement with, digital media. This new reality has given our project—and this book—its particular focus. Though our project set out to explore literacy, the young people we worked with quickly taught us that *learning* is the more significant and relevant aspect of their lives. For them, learning was variously self-directed, peer-based, observational, experimental and often playful. They learned by observing, sometimes by trial and error and other times from mentors and experts. Most importantly they learned by doing. Literacy, in its many forms, grew out of these processes. But we want to emphasise that our findings should not be seen to suggest a devaluing of more traditional course-based approaches to media training or literacy learning, especially practice-based approaches. We have seen that these approaches can be enormously valuable if the emphasis is on learning.

While our work came to emphasise the need to better understand and support those who do not or who may not be willing or able to participate in courses, we believe our findings are relevant for pedagogical design and delivery. Indeed, there is ample evidence that adult literacy courses, like the learning spaces we described, are most effective when learning is underpinned by recognition of personal histories and the social and cultural environments in which people

positive identity formation and some form of economic enterprise. For many young people who have dropped out of formal education in their early teens, participating in this kind of alternative learning pathway can be a stepping stone to re-entering the formal education and training system. It is clear that through engaging in the youth-oriented programs and projects outlined here many young people have acquired confidence, initiative, aspirations, intellectual and creative energy and skills. Further, they have demonstrated the capacity for reflection and perfection that can be taken into further training, employment and enterprise generation, as well as future leadership roles.

ICTs are clearly generating unique opportunities for Indigenous youth and creating a new generation skilled in digital technologies.[1] While only a small number of young people may be employed in the ICT industry, developing competence in this domain will have a ripple effect in the employment domains of arts centres, land management, ranger programs, health, environmental health, community history research and archiving, radio and TV broadcasting, and the Australian film industry, as well as academic research.

live. Those personal and local contexts are vitally important in the ways they shape options and capacities for learning (Chodkiewicz, et al. 2010). Paradoxically, it has been shown that literacy is more likely to grow if literacy itself is not over emphasised and people's life projects are the focus of activity (Barton 2009:57). This is confirmed in our observation of the many meaningful and productive learning activities carried out in the communities and among the young people we worked with.

We recognise that our call to emphasise learning over formal teaching and training raises some serious problems for policy makers. In contravention to the growing demands for 'skills' and 'evidence-based' policy, the successful learning we observed was often inconspicuous or invisible, and the outcomes typically could not be 'captured in terms of short-term quantifiable gains' (Cuban 2009: 13). This suggests to us the need to acknowledge 'soft outcomes' such as gains in self-esteem, personal development, confidence, motivation, collaboration and problem-solving (Barton 2009: 56). It also highlights the need to incorporate locally-specific indicators of program or project success

As has been observed elsewhere, policies and public investments in literacy curriculum and pedagogy are almost always rationalised in terms of measurable impact on literacy proficiency. If literacy proficiency does not immediately increase, programs are often judged a failure. Yet research shows that gains in literacy proficiency seldom appear overnight. Rather, programs that support high levels of engagement

leading to increased literacy practice result in the long term in higher levels of proficiency (Reder 2009:47). Though our research did not address formal adult literacy instruction, those findings have a deep resonance with our observations that meaningful engagement with practice—with productive learning—and the 'soft outcomes' it yields, may lead to greater proficiency in a number of domains in adult life.

In addition, our research shows that the pathway to meaningful outcomes sometimes may be slow, but that each learning experience incrementally builds up the skill-base of the individual and contributes to the development of collective expertise over the long-term. This collective expertise is also very difficult to quantify and measure, yet it is clear that it is a crucial element for catalysing young people in productive learning and for the development of community engagement, enterprise (including employment) and ultimately community leadership. Significant too is the way in which all these successful young people become role models and provide a new sense of possibility for successive generations to aspire to.

In conclusion, if Indigenous young people are to become competent, mature adults able to shape their own futures and the economic and social viability of their communities, then attention will need to be paid not only to institutional education and training pathways, but also to other approaches to productive learning that will contribute to the formation of a positive sense of self, strong cultural identities and the learning and literacy skills needed to shape Indigenous futures. The challenge for all of us is to find ways to design and support these various and exciting forms of productive learning. We hope this book will be a contribution toward meeting that challenge.

Chapter 5 endnotes

1. Statement on Key Issues, ITIC Symposium, 13–15 July, Canberra. Available at: **http://www.aiatsis.gov.au/research/symposia/Digi10.html**

APPENDIX 1
Relevant weblinks

AUSTRALIA

Project links

CAEPR – Youth Learning
http://caepr.anu.edu.au/youth/index.php

Djilpin Arts
http://www.djilpinarts.org.au/

Ngaanyatjarra Media
http://www.waru.org/organisations/ngmedia/

Ngapartji Ngapartji
http://www.ngapartji.org/
http://www.bighart.org/public/

Northern Territory Library remote community
Libraries and Knowledge Centres
http://www.ntl.nt.gov.au/about_us/knowledgecentre

PAW Media and Communications
http://www.pawmedia.com.au/

The Fred Hollows Foundation
http://www.hollows.org.au/Page.aspx?ID=2145

Warlpiri Youth Development/
Mt Theo Youth Program
http://www.mttheo.org/home/

Warlpiri Education and Training Trust
http://www.clc.org.au/Building_the_bush/wett.html

Other

Alice Springs Public Library
http://www.alicesprings.nt.gov.au/library

Carclew Youth Arts
http://www.carclew.com.au/Program/
PublicOutreachPrograms

Circosis
http://www.circosis.com.au/

Community Prophets youth media projects
http://www.communityprophets.com/
http://www.abc.net.au/usmob/

Crossing Roper Bar – Australian Art Orchestra
http://aao.com.au/projects/programs/program/
crossing-roper-bar/

Martu Media and CuriousWorks
http://www.martumedia.com.au/
http://www.curiousworks.com.au/tag/martu/

Mulka Project
http://www.mulka.org/themulkaproject

Music Outback
http://www.musicoutback.com.au/

NPY Women's Council Youth Programs
http://www.npywc.org.au/html/youth.html

Pelican Project
http://www.svpelican.com.au/pages/stories.html

Photo Me Project, Derby WA
http://www.sidebyside.net.au/gallery/
    main.php?g2_itemId=24
http://www.sidebyside.net.au/

Slipprysirkus
http://www.slipprysirkus.org/

Tangentyere Council Youth Programs
http://www.tangentyere.org.au/services/
    family_youth/caylus/
http://www.tangentyere.org.au/services/
    family_youth/drum_atweme/

Wilurarra Creative
(Warburton Youth Arts Project)
http://wilurarra.com/

INTERNATIONAL

Youth arts

http://www.afhboston.com/

http://www.riverzedgearts.org/

http://www.americansforthearts.org/youtharts/

Community ICT projects

http://www.projetoclicar.org.br/

http://www.computerclubhouse.org/about1.htm

http://harlemlive.org/index.php

http://asasdobeijaflor.blogspot.com/

http://www.pbs.org/frontlineworld/stories/india/
    kids.html

http://www.hole-in-the-wall.com/

http://novo.vivafavela.com.br/publique/cgi/cgilua.exe/
    sys/start.htm?infoid=40489&sid=74

http://www.storycenter.org/index1.html

http://www.space2cre8.com/

Language and literacy strategies to support ICT and digital media activities

Providing literacy, ICT and digital media support is often difficult for facilitators who work with youth in non-formal learning environments such as those described in this book. New media is, however, an integral, yet often unrecognised facet of work with Indigenous youth. In this light we offer a few useful language and literacy strategies.

VOLUNTEERS

Organisations may consider engaging volunteers as support workers. The following organisations can be contacted for more information:

▶ Indigenous Community Volunteers
  http://www.icv.com.au/

▶ Youth Challenge Australia
  http://www.youthchallenge.org.au/
  Central-Australia

Even without additional support, facilitators may consider some of the following strategies.

SCAFFOLDING

Providing assistance and support to aid learning, literacy and independent engagement with ICTs and online media activities:

▶ **ENLARGE FONT SIZES ON COMPUTER SCREENS**
  Font sizes on computer screens are often too small for people with poor eyesight.

▶ **ICONS**
  Users typically use visual-spatial references and icon-based navigation to complete actions on the computer screen. Many can be figured out intuitively. However some icons or symbols may need to be 'decoded'. These could be identified on a handy chart posted nearby the computer/s.

▶ **SHORTCUTS**
  As computer users become more proficient they will need to know how to use 'shortcuts'. Create a chart of the most common shortcuts for Macs and PCs. For example:

COMMAND	MAC	PC
Copy	Command [⌘] + C	CTRL + C
Cut	Command [⌘] + X	CTRL + X
Paste	Command [⌘] + V	CTRL + V

▶ **SAVE > SAVE AS (new name)**
  Teach people how to do 'Save As' > new name. Many users use the same name for new documents or files (eg in Word or new projects in *GarageBand*) and accidentally override previous saves.

▶ **SEARCH WORDS and ALPHABETICAL LISTS**
  Users may have trouble searching for specific information (e.g. in *Google* or in *Ara Irititja*) because they don't know how to spell words or cannot discriminate between similar listed words, that is, they tend to follow links between sites rather than search for specific information/sites.

Such searches require accurate spelling AND an ability to read through words or fields listed in alphabetical order to find the correct search item.

To assist users:

i. A reference list of predictable search words with the correct spelling can be listed next to the computer.

ii. Teach users how to skim through lists and predict correct choices.

iii. When searching for specific information, e.g. for a 'used car', it is useful to understand how to enter required information, often in an abbreviated forms, e.g. min/max price range, make/model, diesel/ petrol etc. To assist users a list chart of predictable categories and/or abbreviations could be made.

▸ **PASSWORDS**

People commonly need a LOG IN customer number/member number/customer ID/email address, plus a password (i.e. for internet banking, *Facebook*, etc). These are easily forgotten, so keep a list in a private and secure location. Remember to tell users to copy passwords carefully, taking care with spaces, underlines and lower/upper case letters.

▸ **CASE SENSITIVE TYPING**

Ensure that users are aware of the difference between upper and lower case letters, and how to use the 'Shift' and 'Caps lock' keys on the keyboard. This is especially relevant when typing in case sensitive passwords.

▸ **INTERNET BANKING**

Teach internet banking in two stages:

i. passive—going into an account and checking the balance.

ii. active—going into an account to transfer money.

▸ **iTunes PLAYLIST**

Make a chart showing users how to make their own playlist. For example, to choose songs according to genre, band or singers, 'Ctrl click' choices and drag them to the playlist.

▸ Burn playlist on CD

▸ Drag to iPod.

▸ **COMPUTER GAMES**

Games are typically learned not by following the written rules, but random pressing of buttons until a 'pattern' emerges. Users can be systematically taught how to find new games on the web or in folders.

SCAFFOLDING THE READING/ WRITING PROCESS

Many multimedia activities involve reading and/ or writing. Young people typically want to label photos, write short texts in films, write songs or transcribe songs. These literacy tasks may be done in English. Young people may ask for assistance from someone who is literate in English, however that person may still need help with writing words and phrases correctly.

To assist users: compile a list of typical words, phrases and place names with the correct spelling and attach the list to the wall.

VERNACULAR LITERACY

It is also commonplace for young people to want to write in their Indigenous mother tongue. Few young people are literate in local Indigenous languages. While it may not be possible to organise vernacular literacy lessons, other strategies will help:

Orthography

The sound system of Aboriginal languages differs from English therefore a different spelling system tends to be used. The orthography is the 'alphabet' or sound/symbol system for the language. You can assist users by placing a language dictionary and/or learners guide in the space for users to access. These resources can also be used to:

i. Find or make an 'alphabet' chart for the wall. Make sure that all diacritics are included (i.e. underlines or other marks attached to letters that indicate how to pronounce the symbol).

ii. Find or make syllable charts.

iii. Find or make charts of predictable key words and place names with correct spelling.

Resources such as dictionaries or learners guides for many Indigenous languages can be purchased. See IAD Press, the Indigenous publishing house in Alice Springs: **http://iadpress.com/**.

Suggestions for further reading

LANGUAGE AND NEW LITERACIES

Alvermann, D. (Ed.) (2002) *Adolescents and literacies in a digital world,* New York: Peter Lang.

Baron, N. S. (2008) *Always on: language in an online and mobile world.* New York: Oxford University Press.

Hull, G. A. (2003) 'At last. Youth culture and digital media: New literacies for new times'. *Research in the Teaching of English,* Vol.38, No.2, pp. 229–233.

Hull, G. A. and Stornaiuolo, A. (2010) 'Literate arts in a global world: Reframing social networking as cosmopolitan practice'. *Journal of Adolescent and Adult Literacy,* Vol.54, No.2, pp. 85–97.

Kress, G. (2003) *Literacy in the new media age.* London and New York: Routledge.

Kress, G. (2010) *Multimodality: A social semiotic approach to contemporary communication.* London and New York: Routledge Taylor and Francis Group.

Soep, E. (2006) 'Beyond literacy and voice in youth media production'. *McGill Journal of Education,* Vol.41, No.3, pp. 197–213.

Tyner, K. (1998) *Literacy in a digital world: Teaching and learning in the age of information.* Mahwah NJ: Lawrence Erlbaum Associates.

Stornaiuolo, A., Hull, G. and Nelson, M. E. (2009) 'Mobile texts and migrant audiences: Rethinking literacy and assessment in a new media age'. *Research directions: Language arts,* Vol.86, No.5, pp. 382–392.

Thurlow, C. and Mroczek, K. (Eds.) (2011) *Digital discourse: Language in the new media,* New York: Oxford University Press.

LITERACY AS SOCIAL PRACTICE

Barton, D., Hamilton, M. and Ivanic, R. (Eds.) (2000) *Situated literacies: Reading and writing in context,* London: Routledge.

Barton, D., Ivanic, R., Appleby, Y., Hodge, R. and Tusting, K. (2007) *Literacy, lives and learning.* London: Routledge.

Gee, J. P. (2004) *Situated language and learning: A critique of traditional schooling.* New York and London: Routledge.

Heath, S. B. (1983) *Ways with words: Language, life and work in communities and classrooms.* Cambridge: Cambridge University Press.

Kral, I. (2012) *Talk, Text & Technology: Literacy and Social Practice in a Remote Indigenous Community.* Clevedon, UK: Multilingual Matters.

Prinsloo, M. and Breier, M. (Eds.) (1996) *The social uses of literacy: Theory and practice in contemporary South Africa,* Amsterdam and Philadelphia: John Benjamins Publishing.

Street, B. V. (Ed.) (1993) *Cross-cultural approaches to literacy,* Cambridge: Cambridge University Press.

DIGITAL MEDIA

Buckingham, D. (2007) *Beyond technology: Children's learning in the age of digital culture.* Malden MA: Polity Press.

Buckingham, D. (Ed.) (2008) *Youth, Identity, and Digital Media.* John D. and Catherine T. MacArthur Foundation Series on Digital Media and Learning. Cambridge, MA: The MIT Press.

Buckingham, D. and Willet, R. (2006) *Digital generations: Children, young people and new media.* London and Mahwah NJ: Lawrence Erlbaum.

Coleman, E. G. (2010) 'Ethnographic approaches to digital media'. *Annual Review of Anthropology,* Vol.39, pp. 487–505.

Ito, M., Baumer, S., Bittanti, M., boyd, d., Cody, R., Herr-Stephenson, B., Horst, H. A., Lange, P. G., Mahendran, D., Martínez, K. Z., Pascoe, C. J., Perkel, D., Robinson, L., Sims, C. and Tripp, L. (2010) *Hanging out, messing around and geeking out: Kids living and learning with new media.* Cambridge, MA and London, England: The MIT Press.

Ginsburg, F. (2008) 'Rethinking the digital age''. In Wilson, P. and Stewart, M. (Eds) *Global Indigenous Media: Cultures, poetics and politics.* Durham and London: Duke University Press, pp. 287–305.

Livingstone, S. (2002) *Young people and new media.* London: Sage.

Osgerby, B. (2004) *Youth media.* New York: Routledge.

Palfrey, J. and Gasser, U. (2008) *Born digital: Understanding the first generation of digital natives.* New York, NY: Basic Books.

Sefton-Green, J. (2006) 'Youth, technology and media cultures'. *Review of Research in Education,* Vol.30, pp. 279–306.

IDENTITY

Alim, H. S., Ibrahim, A. and Pennycook, A. (2009) *Global linguistic flows: hip hop cultures, youth identities, and the politics of language.* New York and Abingdon UK: Routledge.

Bartlett, L. (2007) 'To seem and to feel: Situated identities and literacy practices'. *Teachers College Record,* Vol.109, No.1, pp. 51–69.

Barton, D., Ivanic, R., Appleby, Y., Hodge, R. and Tusting, K. (2007) *Literacy, lives and learning.* London: Routledge.

Bottrell, D. (2007) 'Resistance, Resilience and Social Identities: Reframing 'Problem Youth' and the Problem of Schooling'. *Journal of Youth Studies,* Vol.10, No.5, pp. 597–616.

Mallan, K., Ashford, B. and Singh, P. (2010) 'Navigating iScapes: Australian Youth Constructing Identities and Social Relations in a Network Society'. *Anthropology & Education Quarterly,* Vol.41, No.3, pp. 264–279.

Pennycook, A. (2003) 'Global Englishes, Rip Slyme, and performativity'. *Journal of Sociolinguistics,* Vol.7, No.4, pp. 513–533.

INDIGENOUS YOUTH

Eickelkamp, U. (Ed.) (2011) *Growing Up in Central Australia: New Anthropological Studies on Aboriginal Childhood and Adolescence.*, Berghahn.

Fietz, P. (2008) 'Socialisation and the shaping of youth identity at Docker River'. In Robinson, G., Eickelkamp, U., Goodnow, J. and Katz, I. (Eds) *Contexts of child development: Culture, policy and intervention.* Darwin: Charles Darwin University Press, pp. 49–58.

Kral, I. (2010a) *Generational change, learning and remote Australian Indigenous youth.* CAEPR Working Paper 68. Canberra: Centre for Aboriginal Economic Policy Research, The Australian National University.

Kral, I. (2010b) *Plugged in Remote Australian Indigenous youth and digital culture.* CAEPR Working Paper 69. Canberra: Centre for Aboriginal Economic Policy Research, The Australian National University.

Kral, I. (2011) 'Youth media as cultural practice: Remote Indigenous youth speaking out loud'. *Australian Aboriginal Studies. Journal of the Australian Institute of Aboriginal and Torres Strait Islander Studies,* Vol. 1, pp. 4–16.

Kral, I. (in press 2012) 'The acquisition of media as cultural practice: Remote Indigenous youth and new digital technologies.' In L. Ormond-Parker, Fforde, C., Corn, A., O'Sullivan, S. and Obata, K. (ed.) *Information Technologies and Indigenous Communities.* Canberra: AIATSIS e-Research, accepted 03/2011.

Malcolm, I. G., Konigsberg, P., Collard, G., Hill, A., Grote, E., Sharifian, F., Kickett, A. and Sahanna, E. (2002) *Umob Deadly: Recognised and unrecognised literacy skills of Aboriginal youth.* Mount Lawley, WA: Centre for Applied Language and Literacy Research and Institute for the Service Professions.

Ray, T. (2007) 'Youth well-being in Central Australia'. In Altman, J. and Hinkson, M. (Eds) *Coercive reconciliation: Stabilise, normalise, exit Aboriginal Australia.* North Carlton, Australia: Arena Publications, pp. 195–203.

ETHNOGRAPHY

Heath, S. B. (1995) 'Ethnography in communities: Learning the everyday life of America's subordinated youth'. In Banks, J. A. and Banks, C. A. M. (Eds) *Handbook of research on multicultural education.* New York: Simon and Schuster Macmillan, pp. 114–128.

Heath, S. B. (1997) 'Culture: Contested realm in research on children and youth'. *Applied Developmental Science,* Vol.1, No.3, pp. 113–123.

Heath, S. B. and Street, B. V. (2008) *On ethnography: Approaches to language and literacy research.* New York, NY: Teachers College Press.

Jessor, R., Colby, A. and Shweder, R. A. (Eds.) (1996) *Ethnography and human development: Context and meaning in social inquiry,* Chicago: The University of Chicago Press.

Wolcott, H. (1985) 'On ethnographic intent'. *Educational Administration Quarterly,* Vol.21, No.3, pp. 187–203.

References

Altman, J. C. (2007) 'Alleviating poverty in remote Indigenous Australia: The role of the hybrid economy'. *CAEPR Topical Issue,* Vol.10, No.2007, pp. 1–9. (An electronic publication downloaded from <http://www.anu.edu.au/caepr/> 23/10/08).

Andrews, G. B., Covic, T., Yeung, A. S., Craven, R. G. and O'Rourke, V. (2008) *Opening the Blind Eye: Causal Modelling of Perceived Discrimination and Academic Disengagement for Indigenous Students.* Unpublished paper given at the Association for Active Educational Researchers International Education Conference: Brisbane 30 November–4 December 2008. Accessed 24 October 2011, <http://ocs.sfu.ca/aare/index.php/AARE_2008/AARE/paper/viewFile/758/129>.

Appadurai, A. (1996) *Modernity at large: Cultural dimensions of globalization.* Minneapolis, Minnesota: University of Minnesota Press.

Austin-Broos, D. (2003) 'Places, practices, and things: The articulation of Arrernte kinship with welfare and work'. *American Ethnologist,* Vol.30, No.1, pp. 118–135.

Australian Institute of Aboriginal and Torres Strait Islander Studies with the Federation of Aboriginal and Torres Strait Islander Languages (2005) *National Indigenous Languages Survey Report 2005.* Canberra: Commonwealth of Australia.

Baron, N. S. (2008) *Always on: language in an online and mobile world.* New York: Oxford University Press.

Barron, B. (2006) 'Interest and self-sustained learning as catalysts of development: A learning ecology framework'. *Human Development,* Vol.49, pp. 193–224.

Bartlett, L. (2007) 'To seem and to feel: Situated identities and literacy practices'. *Teachers College Record,* Vol.109, No.1, pp. 51–69.

Bartlett, L. and Holland, D. (2002) 'Theorizing the space of literacy practices'. *Ways of Knowing Journal,* Vol.2, No.1, pp. 10–22.

Barton, D., Ivanic, R., Appleby, Y., Hodge, R. and Tusting, K. (2007) *Literacy, lives and learning.* London: Routledge.

Bauman, R. and Briggs, C. L. (1990) 'Poetics and performance as critical perspectives on language and social life'. *Annual Review of Anthropology,* Vol.19, pp. 59–88.

Bottrell, D. (2007) 'Resistance, Resilience and Social Identities: Reframing 'Problem Youth' and the Problem of Schooling'. *Journal of Youth Studies,* Vol.10, No.5, pp. 597–616.

Bottrell, D. and Armstrong, D. (2007) 'Changes and exchanges in marginal youth transitions'. *Journal of Youth Studies,* Vol.10, No.3, pp. 353–371.

Bourdieu, P. (1984) *Distinction: a social critique of the judgement of taste.* London: Routledge and Kegan Paul.

Brady, M. (1992) *Heavy metal: The social meaning of petrol sniffing in Australia.* Canberra: Aboriginal Studies Press.

Brooks, D. (2011) 'Organization within disorder: The present and future of young people in the Ngaanyatjarra Lands'. In Eickelkamp, U. and Fietz, P. (Eds) *Youngfella World: Indigenous Experiences of Childhood and Youth in Central Australia.* Oxford:: Berghahn Books, pp. 183–212.

Bucholtz, M. (2002) 'Youth and cultural practice'. *Annual Review of Anthropology,* Vol.31, pp. 525–552.

Buckingham, D. (2008a) 'Introducing Identity'. In Buckingham, D. (Ed.) *Youth, Identity, and Digital Media. John D. and Catherine T. MacArthur Foundation Series on Digital Media and Learning.* Cambridge, MA: The MIT Press, pp. 1–22.

Buckingham, D. (Ed.) (2008b) *Youth, Identity, and Digital Media.,* John D. and Catherine T. MacArthur Foundation Series on Digital Media and Learning. Cambridge, MA: The MIT Press.

Burbank, V. (1988) *Aboriginal adolescence: maidenhood in an Australian community.* New Brunswick: Rutgers University Press.

Burbank, V. (2006) 'From bedtime to on time: Why many Aboriginal people don't especially like participating in Western institutions'. *Anthropological Forum,* Vol.16, No.1, pp. 3–20.

Cammarota, J. (2008) 'The cultural organising of youth ethnographers: Formalising a praxis-based ethnography'. *Anthropology & Education Quarterly,* Vol.39, No.1, pp. 45–58.

Chodkiewicz, A., Widin, J. and Yasukawa, K. (2010) 'Making Connections to Re-engage Young People in Learning: Dimensions of Practice'. *Literacy & Numeracy Studies,* Vol.18, No.1, pp. 35–51.

Coates, S., Fitzpatrick, L., McKenna, A. and Makin, A. (1995) *National Reporting System: A mechanism for reporting outcomes of adult English language, literacy and numeracy programs.* Melbourne: ANTA and DEET.

Corbett, M. (2004) '"It was fine, if you wanted to leave": Educational ambivalence in a Nova Scotian coastal community 1963–1998'. *Anthropology and Education Quarterly,* Vol.35, No.4, pp. 451–471.

Coy, M. W. (Ed.) (1989) *Apprenticeship: From Theory to Method and Back Again,* Albany, NY: SUNY Press.

Crystal, D. (2008) *Txtng: The Gr8 Db8.* Oxford: Oxford University Press.

Cuban, S. (2009) 'Outside Practices: Learning within the borderlands'. *Literacy & Numeracy Studies,* Vol.16.2/17.1, No.1, pp. 5–18.

Cushman, E. and Emmons, C. (2002) 'Contact zones made real'. In Hull, G. and Schultz, K. (Eds) *School's out!: Bridging out-of-school literacies with classroom practice.* Columbia University NY: Teachers College Press, pp. 203–232.

Daly, A. E. (2005) *Bridging the Digital Divide: The Role of Community Online Access Centres in Indigenous Communities.* Discussion Paper 273: Centre for Aboriginal Economic Policy Research, ANU Canberra.

Deger, J. (2006) *Shimmering screens: Making media in an Aboriginal community.* Minneapolis and London: University of Minnesota Press.

Duff, P. and Hornberger, N. (Eds.) (2008) *Language Socialization: Encyclopedia of Language and Education, Volume 8,* New York: Springer.

Duff, P. A. (2008) 'Introduction'. In Duff, P. and Hornberger, N. (Eds) *Language Socialization: Encyclopedia of Language and Education, Volume 8.* New York: Springer, pp. xiii–xix.

Dyson, L. E., Hendriks, M. and Grant, S. (Eds.) (2007) *Information technologies and Indigenous people.,* London and Melbourne: Information Science Publishing.

Eickelkamp, U. (Ed.) (2011) *Growing Up in Central Australia: New Anthropological Studies of Aboriginal Childhood and Adolescence.,* New York and Oxford: Berghahn Books.

Eidman-Aadahl, E. (2002) 'Got some time, got a place, got the word: Collaborating for literacy learning and youth development'. In Hull, G. and Schultz, K. (Eds) *School's out!: Bridging out-of-school literacies with classroom practice.* Columbia University NY: Teachers College Press, pp. 241–260.

Engeström, Y. (1987) *Learning by Expanding: An Activity Theoretical Approach to Developmental Research.* Helsinki: Orienta Konsultit.

Featherstone, D. (2011) 'The Ngaanyatjarra Lands Telecommunication Project: A Quest for Broadband in the Western Desert'. *Telecommunications Journal of Australia,* Vol.61, No.1, pp. 4.1–4.25.

Fietz, P. (2008) 'Socialisation and the shaping of youth identity at Docker River'. In Robinson, G., Eickelkamp, U., Goodnow, J. and Katz, I. (Eds) *Contexts of child development: Culture, policy and intervention.* Darwin: Charles Darwin University Press, pp. 49–58.

Fluehr-Lobban, C. (2008) 'Collaborative Anthropology as Twenty-first-Century Ethical Anthropology'. *Collaborative Anthropologies,* Vol.1, pp. 175–182.

Fogarty, W. (2010) *'Learning through Country': Competing knowledge systems and place based pedagogy.* Unpublished PhD (Anthropology), Canberra: The Australian National University.

Garrett, P. B. and Baquedano-Lopez, P. (2002) 'Language socialization: Reproduction and continuity, transformation and change'. *Annual Review of Anthropology,* Vol.31, pp. 339–361.

Gee, J. P. (2003) *What video games have to teach us about learning and literacy.* New York: Palgrave Macmillan.

Gee, J. P. (2004) *Situated language and learning: A critique of traditional schooling.* New York and London: Routledge.

Gee, J. P. (2005) 'Semiotic social spaces and affinity spaces'. In Barton, D. and Tusting, K. (Eds) *Beyond communities of practice: Language, power and social context.* Cambridge: Cambridge University Press, pp. 214–232.

Gibson, J. (2007) *People, place and community memory: Creating digital heritage databases in remote Aboriginal communities.* Initiatives, ideas and interaction: Sharing our story Conference, 2007. Alice Springs: Australian Society of Archivists Inc.

Gibson, J., Lloyd, B. and Richmond, C. (2011) 'Localisation of Indigenous content: Libraries and Knowledge Centres and the Our Story Database in the Northern Territory'. In Steyn, J., van Belle, J.-P. and Mansilla, E., V (Eds) *ICTs for global development and sustainability: Practice and applications.* Hershey and New York: Information Science Reference, pp. 151–175.

Goodale, J. C. (1971) *Tiwi wives: A study of the women of Melville Island, North Australia.* Seattle and London: University of Washington Press.

Goodwin, C. (2000) 'Action and embodiment within situated human interaction'. *Journal of Pragmatics,* Vol.32, pp. 1489–1522.

Greenfield, P. M. (2009) 'Technology and Informal Education: What is Taught, What is Learned.' *Science,* Vol.323, pp. 69–71.

Gumperz, J. J. and Hymes, D. (1972) *Directions in sociolinguistics: The ethnography of communication.* New York: Holt, Rinehart and Winston.

Hamilton, A. (1981) *Nature and nurture: Aboriginal child-rearing in North-Central Arnhem Land.* Canberra: Australian Institute of Aboriginal Studies.

Handleman, D. (1990) *Models and Mirrors: Towards an Anthropology of Public Events.* Cambridge: Cambridge University Press.

Heath, S. B. (1983) *Ways with words: Language, life and work in communities and classrooms.* Cambridge: Cambridge University Press.

Heath, S. B. (1990) 'The children of Trackton's children: Spoken and written language in social change'. In Stigler, J. W., Shweder, R. A. and Herdt, G. (Eds) *Cultural psychology: Essays on comparative human development.* Cambridge: Cambridge University Press, pp. 496–519.

Heath, S. B. (1997) 'Culture: Contested realm in research on children and youth'. *Applied Developmental Science,* Vol.1, No.3, pp. 113–123.

Heath, S. B. (1998) 'Working through language'. In Hoyle, S. M. and Adger, S. T. (Eds) *Kids talk: Strategic language use in later childhood.* New York and Oxford: Oxford University Press, pp. 217–240.

Heath, S. B. (2007) *Diverse learning and learner diversity in "informal" science learning environments.* Paper prepared for National Research Council's Board on Science Education for Learning in Informal Environments Study. March 30 2007.

Heath, S. B. (2008) 'Language socialization in the learning communities of adolescents'. In Duff, P. and Hornberger, N. (Eds) *Language Socialization, Vol. 8, Encyclopedia of Language and Education. 2nd. Ed.* New York: Springer, pp. 217–230.

Heath, S. B. (2010) *Artful Science: How the young learn by looking, imitating, acting, modeling, having real roles, and through 'memories of the future'.* The Australian National University, Canberra: Toyota ANU Public Lecture Series. February 23, 2010.

Heath, S. B. and McLaughlin, M. W. (Eds.) (1993) *Identity and inner-city youth: Beyond ethnicity and gender.,* Columbia NY: Teachers College Press.

Heath, S. B. and Smyth, L. (1999) *ArtShow: Youth and community development. A resource guide.* Washington: Partners for a livable community.

Heath, S. B. and Street, B. V. (2008) *On ethnography: Approaches to language and literacy research.* New York, NY: Teachers College Press.

Hirschfeld, L. A. (2002) 'Why don't anthropologists like children?' *American Anthroplogist,* Vol.104, No.2, pp. 611–627.

Hoyle, S. M. and Adger, S. T. (Eds.) (1998) *Kids Talk: Strategic language use in later childhood,* New York and Oxford: Oxford University Press.

Hughes, M. and Dallwitz, J. (2007) 'Ara Irititja: Towards culturally appropriate IT best practice in remote Indigenous Australia'. In Dyson, L. E., Hendriks, M. and Grant, S. (Eds) *Information technologies and Indigenous people*. London and Melbourne: Information Science Publishing, pp. 146–158.

Hull, G. and Schultz, K. (Eds.) (2002) *School's out! Bridging out-of-school literacies with classroom practice,* Columbia University, NY: Teachers College Press.

Hull, G. A. (2003) 'At last. Youth culture and digital media: New literacies for new times'. *Research in the Teaching of English,* Vol.38, No.2, pp. 229–233.

Hull, G. A. and Nelson, M. E. (2005) 'Locating the semiotic power of multimodality'. *Written Communication,* Vol.22, No.2, pp. 224–261.

Indigenous Remote Communications Association (2010) *Joining the dots: Dreaming a digital future for remote Indigenous communities.* Indigenous Remote Communications Association (IRCA) submission to the Indigenous Broadcasting and Media Sector Review. Submission Date: 31st August 2010. Accessed 18 January 2011, <http://remotemedia.wikispaces.com/>.

Ito, M., Baumer, S., Bittanti, M., boyd, d., Cody, R., Herr-Stephenson, B., Horst, H. A., Lange, P. G., Mahendran, D., Martínez, K. Z., Pascoe, C. J., Perkel, D., Robinson, L., Sims, C. and Tripp, L. (2010) *Hanging out, messing around and geeking out: Kids living and learning with new media.* Cambridge, MA and London, England: The MIT Press.

Jessor, R., Colby, A. and Shweder, R. A. (Eds.) (1996) *Ethnography and human development: Context and meaning in social inquiry,* Chicago: The University of Chicago Press.

Jones, G. M. and Schieffelin, B. B. (2009) 'Talking text and talking back: "My BFF Jill" from Boob Tube to YouTube'. *Journal of Computer-Mediated Communication,* Vol.14, pp. 1050–1079.

Jones, R. H. (2010) 'Cyberspace and physical space: Attention structures in computer mediated communication.' In Jaworski, A. and Thurlow, C. (Eds) *Semiotic Landscapes: Language, Image, Space.* London: Continuum, pp. 151–167.

Katz, C. (2004) *Growing up global: Economic restructuring and children's everyday lives.* Minneapolis and London: University of Minnesota Press.

Kral, I. (2010a) *Generational change, learning and remote Australian Indigenous youth.* CAEPR Working Paper 68. Canberra: Centre for Aboriginal Economic Policy Research, The Australian National University.

Kral, I. (2010b) *Plugged in Remote Australian Indigenous youth and digital culture.* CAEPR Working Paper 69. Canberra: Centre for Aboriginal Economic Policy Research, The Australian National University.

Kral, I. (2011a) 'Technology dreaming'. *Arts Yarn Up,* Australia Council for the Arts, Autumn, pp. 12–14.

Kral, I. (2011b) 'Youth media as cultural practice: Remote Indigenous youth speaking out loud'. *Australian Aboriginal Studies. Journal of the Australian Institute of Aboriginal and Torres Strait Islander Studies,* Vol.1, pp. 4–16.

Kral, I. (2012) *Talk, text and technology: Literacy and social practice in a remote Indigenous community.* Bristol, Buffalo, Toronto: Multilingual Matters.

Kral, I. and Falk, I. (2004) *What is all that learning for?: Indigenous adult English literacy practices, training, community capacity and health.* Adelaide: NCVER.

Kral, I. and Schwab, R. G. (2003) *The realities of Indigenous adult literacy acquisition and practice: Implications for remote community capacity development.* CAEPR Discussion Paper No.257. Canberra: The Australian National University.

Kress, G. (2003) *Literacy in the new media age.* London and New York: Routledge.

Kress, G. (2010) *Multimodality: A social semiotic approach to contemporary communication.* London and New York: Routledge Taylor and Francis Group.

Lave, J. (1988) *Cognition in practice.* Cambridge: Cambridge University Press.

Lave, J. (1990) 'The culture of acquisition and the practice of understanding'. In Stigler, J. W., Shweder, R. A. and Herdt, G. (Eds) *Cultural psychology: Essays on comparative human development.* Cambridge: Cambridge University Press, pp. 309–327.

Lave, J. (2011) *Apprenticeship in Critical Ethnographic Practice.* Chicago: University of Chicago Press.

Lave, J. and Wenger, E. (1991) *Situated learning: Legitimate peripheral participation.* Cambridge: Cambridge University Press.

Leonard, J. (2008) *Alternative learning pathways: Community based approaches.* Alice Springs: Presentation by Jane Leonard for Ngapartji Ngapartji, 'Learning for Desert Futures', Desert Knowledge Symposium.

Livingstone, S. (2002) *Young people and new media.* London: Sage.

Malinowski, B. (1963) *The family among the Australian Aborigines.* New York: Shocken Books.

Mallan, K., Ashford, B. and Singh, P. (2010) 'Navigating iScapes: Australian Youth Constructing Identities and Social Relations in a Network Society'. *Anthropology & Education Quarterly,* Vol.41, No.3, pp. 264–279.

McCarty, T. L. and Wyman, L. T. (2009) 'Indigenous youth and bilingualism: Theory, research, praxis'. *Journal of Language, Identity, and Education,* Vol.8, pp. 279–290.

McKendrick, J., Scott, G. and Sinclair, S. (2007) 'Dismissing disaffection: Young people's attitudes towards education, employment and participation in a deprived community'. *Journal of Youth Studies,* Vol.10, No.2, pp. 139–160.

McLaughlin, M. W., Irby, M. A. and Langman, J. (1994) *Urban sanctuaries: Neighborhood organizations in the lives and futures of inner-city youths.* San Francisco CA: Jossey-Bass Publishers.

Merlan, F. (1998) *Caging the rainbow: Places, politics and Aborigines in a north Australian town.* Honolulu: University of Hawai'i Press.

Ormond-Parker, L., Fforde, C., Corn, A., O'Sullivan, S. and Obata, K. (Eds.) (2012) *Information Technologies and Indigenous Communities,* Canberra: AIATSIS e-Research, accepted 03/2011.

Paradise, R. and Rogoff, B. (2009) 'Side by side: Learning by observing and pitching in'. *Ethos,* Vol.37, No.1, pp. 102–138.

Pearson, N. (2000) *Our right to take responsibility.* Cairns: Noel Pearson and Associates.

Pennycook, A. (2003) 'Global Englishes, Rip Slyme, and performativity'. *Journal of Sociolinguistics,* Vol.7, No.4, pp. 513–533.

Rennie, E., Crouch, A., Thomas, J. and Taylor, P. (2010) 'Beyond Public Access? Reconsidering Broadband for Remote Indigenous Communities.''. *Communication, Politics and Culture,* Vol.43, No.1, pp. 48–69.

Rennie, E. and Featherstone, D. (2008) 'The Potential Diversity of Things We Call TV: Indigenous Community Television, self-determination and the advent of NITV'. *Media International Australia incorporating culture and policy,* Vol.129, pp. 52–66.

Robinson, G. (1990) 'Separation, retaliation and suicide: Mourning and the conflicts of young Tiwi men'. *Oceania,* Vol.60, No.3, pp. 161–178.

Rogoff, B. (1990) *Apprenticeship in thinking: Cognitive development in social context.* Oxford: Oxford University Press.

Rogoff, B., Paradise, R., Arauz, R. M., Correa-Chavez, M. and Angelillo, C. (2003) 'Firsthand learning through intent participation'. *Annual Review of Psychology,* Vol.54, pp. 175–203.

Rothbauer, P. M., Walter, V. A. and Weibel, K. (2011) 'Public libraries in the lives of young readers: Past, present and future'. In S. A. Wolf, K. Coats, P. Enciso and Jenkins, C. A. (Eds) *Handbook of research on children's and young adult literature.* New York and Abingdon, England: Routledge, pp. 134–147.

Sandefur, J. R. (1979) *An Australian Creole in the Northern Territory: a description of Ngukurr-Bamyili dialects (Part 1).* Darwin, NT: Australian Aborigines Branch, Summer Institute of Linguistics.

Schieffelin, B. B. and Ochs, E. (Eds.) (1986) *Language socialization across cultures,* Cambridge: Cambridge University Press.

Schwab, R. G. (1999) *Only One in Three? The Complex Reasons for Low Indigenous School Retention.* CAEPR Research Monograph 16, Canberra: The Centre for Aboriginal Economic Policy Research, The Australian National University.

Schwab, R. G. (2001) ''That school gotta recognise *our* policy!': The appropriation of educational policy in an Australian Aboriginal community.' In Sutton, M. and Levinson, B. A. U. (Eds) *Policy as practice: Toward a comparative sociocultural analysis of educational policy.* Westport CT: Ablex, pp. 243–264.

Schwab, R. G. (2012) 'Indigenous early school leavers: Failure, risk and high-stakes testing'. *Australian Aboriginal Studies,* Vol.1, pp. 3–18.

Seely Brown, J. (1999) *Learning, Working & Playing in the Digital Age.* AAHE 1999 Conference on Higher Education. Accessed 20 June 2011, <**www.ntlf.com/ html/sf/jsbrown.pdf**>.

Sefton-Green, J. (2006) 'Youth, technology and media cultures'. *Review of Research in Education,* Vol.30, pp. 279–306.

Simpson, J. and Wigglesworth, G. (Eds.) (2008) *Children's language and multilingualism: Indigenous language use at home and school,* London and New York: Continuum.

Singleton, J. (1999) 'Reflecting on the Reflections: Where Did We Come From? Where Are We Going?' *Anthropology & Education Quarterly,* Vol.30, No.4, pp. 455–459.

Smyth, J. and Hattam, R. (2004) *'Dropping out', drifting off, being excluded: Becoming somebody without school.* New York: Peter Lang.

Soep, E. (2006) 'Beyond literacy and voice in youth media production'. *McGill Journal of Education,* Vol.41, No.3, pp. 197–213.

Stornaiuolo, A., Hull, G. and Nelson, M. E. (2009) 'Mobile texts and migrant audiences: Rethinking literacy and assessment in a new media age'. *Research directions: Language arts,* Vol.86, No.5, pp. 382–392.

Street, B. V. (1995) *Social literacies: Critical approaches to literacy in development, ethnography and education.* London and New York: Longman.

Summerson Carr, E. (2010) 'Enactments of Expertise'. *Annual Review of Anthropology,* Vol.39, pp. 17–32.

Tannock, S. (1998) 'Noisy Talk: Conversation and collaboration in a youth writing group'. In Hoyle, S. M. and Adger, S. T. (Eds) *Kids Talk: Strategic language use in later childhood.* New York and Oxford: Oxford University Press, pp. 241–265.

Teale, W. and Sulzby, E. (1986) *Emergent literacy: Writing and reading.* Norwood, NJ: Ablex.

Thomas, D. and Seely Brown, J. (2009) 'Why Virtual Worlds Can Matter'. *International Journal of Learning and Media,* Vol.1, No.1, pp. 37–49.

Thurlow, C. and Mroczek, K. (Eds.) (2011) *Digital discourse: Language in the new media,* New York: Oxford University Press.

Tonkinson, R. (1978) *The Mardudjara Aborigines: Living the dream in Australia's desert.* New York: Holt, Rinehart and Winston Inc.

Tonkinson, R. (2007) 'Aboriginal 'Difference' and 'Autonomy' then and now: Four decades of change in a Western Desert Society'. *Anthropological Forum,* Vol.17, No.1, pp. 41–60.

Vygotsky, L. S. (1978) *Mind in society: The development of higher psychological processes.* Cambridge MA: Harvard University Press.

Warlpiri Education and Training Trust (2010) 'WETT Youth and Media Program'. *Community Development in Central Australia. Central Land Council: Alice Springs,* Vol.June 2010, p. 7.

Wells, G. (1985) 'Pre-school literacy related activities and success in school'. In Olson, D. R., Torrance, N. and Hildyard, A. (Eds) *Literacy, language and learning: The nature and consequences of reading and writing.* Cambridge: Cambridge University Press, pp. 229–255.

Wenger, E. (1998) *Communities of practice: Learning, meaning and identity.* Cambridge: Cambridge University Press.

Wenger, E., McDermott, R. and Snyder, W. (2002) *Cultivating communities of practice: A guide to managing knowledge.* Cambridge, MA: Harvard Business School Press.

Wertsch, J. V. (1985) *Vygotsky and the social formation of mind.* Cambridge MA: Harvard University Press.

Wyn, J., Cuervo, H., Woodman, D. and Stokes, H. (2005) *Young people, well being and communication technologies.* Melbourne: VicHealth. Accessed 10 February 2011, <http://www.vichealth. vic.gov.au/~/media/ ProgramsandProjects/ MentalHealthandWellBeing/ Publications/Attachments/ Young_People_and_ Technology_Report.ashx>.

Index

www.ingramcontent.com/pod-product-compliance
Lightning Source LLC
Chambersburg PA
CBHW061239270326
41926CB00075B/4681